MURDER

AND

MAYHEM

IN THE HOLY CITY

MURDER

AND

MAYHEM

IN THE HOLY CITY

PAT HENDRIX

WITH CONTRIBUTIONS BY HEATHER SPIRES,
TONI HENDRIX AND JUDY CORBETT

THE
History
PRESS

Published by The History Press
Charleston, SC 29403
www.historypress.net

Cover image by Nick Hendrix.

First published 2006

Manufactured in the United States

ISBN 978.1.59629.162.1

Library of Congress Cataloging-in-Publication Data

Hendrix, Patrick M.
Murder and mayhem in the holy city / Patrick M. Hendrix.
p. cm.
Includes bibliographical references.
ISBN 978-1-59629-162-1 (alk. paper)
1. Crime--South Carolina--Charleston--History. I. Title.
HV6795.C395H46 2006
364.109757'915--dc22
2006013547

CONTENTS

ACKNOWLEDGEMENTS

Now that it is in the final stages, I have been encouraged by the responses of those who have read this manuscript. Your feedback has made it all worthwhile. Without your comments, insights and gentle guidance, it would not have developed the way it has. Though your advice made this manuscript immeasurably better, any mistakes are mine alone.

To help the reader better understand this work, I have included as many sketches as my publisher would allow. On this front, I would like to give thanks to Holly Gleaton, Sandra Hayden, Andrew Richardson and Austin Bunn. You will quickly discover that their work is far better than the writing. My brother, Nick Hendrix, helped draw many of the sketches and was supportive throughout.

I would also like to give thanks to a number of people who have contributed to this work. Edward Fennell from the *Post and Courier* was very generous to give his time and expertise on this very gruesome subject. Toni Hendrix and Judy Corbett came on board as soon as I started working on the manuscript and provided the chapter on the Dawson murder. The chapter on the Six Mile House was written by Heather Spires the day before the manuscript was due. It makes me wonder why she didn't just write the whole thing in ten days. She also served as the editor for the remaining chapters. Thanks to her careful reading and incisive criticism, I was able to produce a better book.

There was as well the type of institutional support without which no work of history would get done. I owe a great deal to the staffs at the Charleston County Public Library, the South Carolina Department of Archives and History and the South Carolina Historical Society. Their knowledge of local history was a godsend. And I give thanks to the other local historians who have worked so hard documenting our shared cultural heritage. Finally, I would like to give praise and thanks to Kirsten Sutton and the staff at The History Press. Their great passion for history and professionalism has made writing this book a pleasure.

INTRODUCTION

L ike the sword of Damocles, death hangs over everyone. No matter how rich, famous, fit or smart, everyone dies. And everyone, it seems, is intrigued by death. Nothing sells as many newspapers, or draws more people to the television and movie theatres than violent death. The more horrifying the death, the more likely people are to be fascinated by it. The phenomenon is undeniable.

The fascination with death did not begin with the modern world. In Ireland, the Celts and their Druid priests combined harvest festivals and changing seasons to celebrate the dead on "Samhain," or "All Hallows." They believed that on October 31, the boundary between the worlds of the living and the dead blurred. They celebrated this night by dancing around huge bonfires and offering sacrifices to the returning dead.

When the Spanish arrived in Mexico, they witnessed elaborate celebrations honoring death and paying homage to Mictecacihuatl, the queen of the underworld. This celebration never really disappeared, but was fused with the Catholic traditions of "All Saints Day" and "All Souls Day" to form "El Dia de Los Muertos," a tradition still celebrated in Mexico today.

It is not just a mythological compulsion that draws people to death. It is also the fascination with murder and murderers. Some believe that the popularization of the murder genre is a sign of cultural degradation, but that's ridiculous. The compulsion has always been with us. People aren't captivated by killing because it's entertainment, although that is sometimes true. Murder brings to the surface the darkest aspects of humanity and gives us a glimpse of a part of human nature that exists in everyone.

If you want to look into the world of murder, South Carolina is as good a place as any to start. This state was statistically one of the most violent places in American history. Though Edgefield County probably takes grand prize as the most murderous place in South Carolina history, Charleston isn't far behind. It is difficult to say exactly why violence was so widespread, but it appears to me to be the combustible combination of cultures and peoples that settled here. Most of these people knew the value of killing before they arrived in Charleston. If you wanted your neighbor's cattle, you killed him and took it. If you wanted land from a neighboring country, you slaughtered the people who lived there and took the land. And if you wanted your neighbors wife, well...you know the rest.

In a larger sense, though, what we witness through Charleston's violent past is the decline of feudal Europe and the wrenching birth of a modern society in the New World. It was not an easy transition. Charleston was an explosive, multiethnic mixture of indifference and greed—a Charles Dickens novel come to life. Most of the immigrants were far from the strapping, well-fed, hard-partying scions of the plantations depicted in Charleston's history. They consisted mainly of tattered, hungry, dirty men and women, many of them half-starved when they arrived. Proud and penniless, these people had to fight it out for everything they got. And fight they did. Persecuted for centuries by European elites, the immigrants would not be bullied in Charleston. They drank harder, fought harder and escalated minor quarrels into murderous frays without a hint of restraint. Vivid descriptions of feuds, brawls, knife fights and murders feature prominently in visitors' accounts, newspaper articles and journals from the eighteenth century onward. The ensuing melees turned the ground red with blood and claimed the lives of countless young men.

While the hooligans brawled in the streets and taverns, gentlemen preferred to duel. To comprehend this practice, one must first understand the culture of Charleston, a culture where violence settled every dispute. When they were not fighting the Native Americans or patrolling for runaway slaves, the sons of the Charleston plantations filled up the dull intervals with whoring, gaming, excessive drinking and anything else that relieved them of thinking. They loved passing whole days and nights at the tavern, and the blood of friends and enemies alike often stained their drunken assemblies. It was only natural that they would embrace dueling. After all, dueling made chivalrous a practice that was nothing more than cold-blooded murder.

Much of the killing featured in this book has nothing to do with historical movements or affairs of honor. Most of the stories reflect the actions of angry boyfriends, thieves, sadists and scoundrels, their choice of weapons as varied as their reasons for killing and maiming. Killing was often done on an intimate level that is hard to imagine in the age of assault rifles and JDAM bombs. Some trampled their enemies from horseback, others used muskets, swords, pistols, knives and even bare hands. The arsenal was varied and the firepower endless. Perhaps Charlestonian James Louis Petigru said it best when he said that "South Carolina is too small for a republic, but too large for an insane asylum." After writing this book, I tend to agree.

THE BLOODY STICK

The sun had been up only a few hours on that fatal spring morning when hundreds of Yamassee warriors descended upon the English colonists in South Carolina, burning settlements and plantations along a wide front in a sudden and fierce attack. So began the Yamassee War of April 15, 1715, which claimed the lives of approximately four hundred colonists and came perilously close to extinguishing the colony of South Carolina.

The attack should have come as no surprise to the English. Since the moment they arrived on the South Carolina coast, the colonists had been heaping abuses on the Indians, kidnapping women and children and driving them off their hunting grounds. The situation had gotten completely out of control, and there were signs that the Native Americans had had enough. Some of the worst offenders were the "Indian traders" that worked the areas south of Charleston. If a Native American was unable to repay his debts, he may have been knocked down, beaten or killed. However, the traders had learned that an Indian was worth more alive than dead: the Barbadians and New Englanders would pay handsomely for an Indian to work their fields. So, as the English moved across the South Carolina landscape, they pursued not only trade but also the Native Americans themselves.

To understand how things had gotten this bad, you would have to look back two hundred years to the arrival of the first Europeans. The Spanish first arrived in the 1520s, and their arrival was like a thunderbolt from a clear blue sky. Lucas Vasquez de Ayllon and a large body of Spanish infantry first landed on the banks of the Combahee River where they were well received by the Native Americans, who offered food and supplies. The Spanish repaid this kindness by inviting 140 Indians aboard their ships, enslaving them and sailing for Cuba. Before reaching their destination, every captive had drowned or died of disease.

Now aware of the Spaniards' predatory intentions, the Native Americans stoutly attacked and nearly annihilated Ayllon's second expedition into coastal South Carolina. Ayllon was followed in 1540 by Hernando de Soto, who passed through South Carolina and visited the great Indian town of Cofitachequi in present-day Kershaw County. The Native American leadership accepted the approach of the enemy without adopting any measures of defense, negotiation or retreat. De Soto was given food, shelter and freshwater pearls by an Indian princess who welcomed the Spanish to the town. Failing to find precious jewels and metals, de Soto decided to push on. Considering it impossible to march through South Carolina without being attacked, he seized the Lady of Cofitachequi and obliged her to issue orders that the Spaniards should be supplied with whatever her territory afforded. She finally escaped near the frontier.

Thereafter, the lands of South Carolina were claimed for Spain and the Catholic Church. There was only one problem: the Native Americans already lived there. If the Spanish wanted to expand their empire at the expense of the Indians, they were going to have to fight—an undertaking they were more than capable and pleased to carry out. After establishing bases, the Spanish pushed into the interior to conduct a vindictive warfare against the local tribes. In a gruesome show of force, armored Spanish mastiffs were used to hunt down and disembowel the Native Americans. Even nursing babies were thrown to these fierce dogs. According to one observer:

> [T]he Spaniards train their fierce dogs to attack, kill and tear to pieces the Indians. It is doubtful that anyone, whether Christian or not, has ever before heard of such a thing as this. The Spaniards keep alive their dogs' appetite for human beings in this way. They have Indians brought to them in chains, then unleash the dogs.

The Indians come meekly down the roads and are killed. And the Spaniards have butcher shops where the corpses of Indians are hung up, on display, and someone will come in and say, more or less, "Give me a quarter of that rascal hanging there, to feed my dogs until I can kill another one for them." As if buying a quarter of a hog or other meat. Other Spaniards go hunting with their dogs in the mornings and when one of them returns at noon and is asked "Did you have good hunting?" he will reply, "Very good! I killed fifteen or twenty rascals and left them with my dogs."

No exact record exists of the number of Native Americans killed or captured by the Spanish Conquistadors, but whatever number that might have been, it was far surpassed by the numbers that were killed by European germs. As the Spanish crossed South Carolina they brought smallpox, measles, bubonic plague and influenza to populations that had no immunity to these infectious pathogens. Epidemics quickly burned through local populations, leaving deserted villages and towns in their wake. Thousands upon thousands perished with not so much as a shot fired. Despite the almost total destruction of their peoples by microbial invaders, the Native Americans engaged the Spanish in a series of protracted and bloody wars. The unremitting attacks diminished the attractions of the Carolina coast in Spanish eyes, and the idea of colonizing it seems to have been permanently abandoned. In 1587, the Spanish burned their homes in South Carolina and withdrew to Florida.

By the time of Charles Towne's founding in 1670, only a few Native American groups could still be found living along the South Carolina coast. These people included the Coosaw, Kiawah, Etiwan and Sewee. The Coosaw inhabited the area to the north and west along the Ashley River. The Kiawah resided at Albemarle Point and along the lower reaches of the Ashley River in 1670, but gave their settlement to the English colonists and moved to Kiawah Island until the early eighteenth century when they moved south of the Combahee River. The Etiwan were settled on or near Daniel Island to the northeast of Charles Towne, but their range extended to the head of the Cooper River. The territory of the Sewee met the territory of the Etiwan high up the Cooper and extended to the north as far as the Santee River. Mortier's map of Carolina, prepared in 1696, shows the Sampas (Sompa) between the Cooper and Wando Rivers, to the northeast of Daniel Island, and the Wando Tribe and Sewel [*sic*] Tribe Fort east of the Wando River, northeast of Daniel Island. Other tribes found outside the Charles Towne area were the Cherokee, the Savannah and the Catawba.

In the first years of settlement, the English colonists were totally dependent on their indigenous neighbors for food and access to the land. In turn, they brought beads and steel knives and whiskey and muskets, but above all they brought disease. The results were apocalyptic. By the early eighteenth century, very few Native Americans could be found near Charles Towne; most had been dispersed or obliterated by disease and the emerging plantation society. The blow was mortal, but they went down fighting.

Though the English treated their neighbors with treachery and disdain, the colonists had avoided a full-scale war with the Native Americans for nearly four decades. They did not yet know it, but their luck was running out. As more settlers moved south of Charles Towne, carving the land into fenced farms and ruining Indian hunting grounds, the colonists began moving into the territory of the Yamassee. Soon thereafter, that fearsome tribe entered into a secret alliance with the Spanish in Florida, who had been unable to dislodge the English from their fortified city. Determined to take back in one stroke what had been lost over forty years, all tribes between Cape Fear and the Gulf of Mexico united in a grand confederacy to annihilate the South Carolina colony. They numbered nine thousand warriors, but their preparations for a general massacre were enveloped in a profound secrecy.

The first certain information concerning an imminent attack came with the breathless arrival of John Fraser, who paddled into Charles Town in a canoe with his wife and child. He informed the authorities that two days before, he had been informed by the Yamassee chief, Sanute, that in a few days "the bloody stick would be sent," and tribes throughout the southeast would simultaneously fall upon the white settlers and no one would be spared. Fraser had been working among the Yamassee for years and refused to believe the danger was real. In order to drive his point home, Sanute told Fraser that when the time came, he would personally kill him and his family rather than let them be burned in the fires of the Yamassee.

Fraser's tale found an audience in Charles Town, where Governor Craven dispatched his best man, Thomas Nairne, to the Yamassee to calm the mounting tensions and "redress all grievances." Nairne had been the colony's Indian agent since 1712 and had spent months living

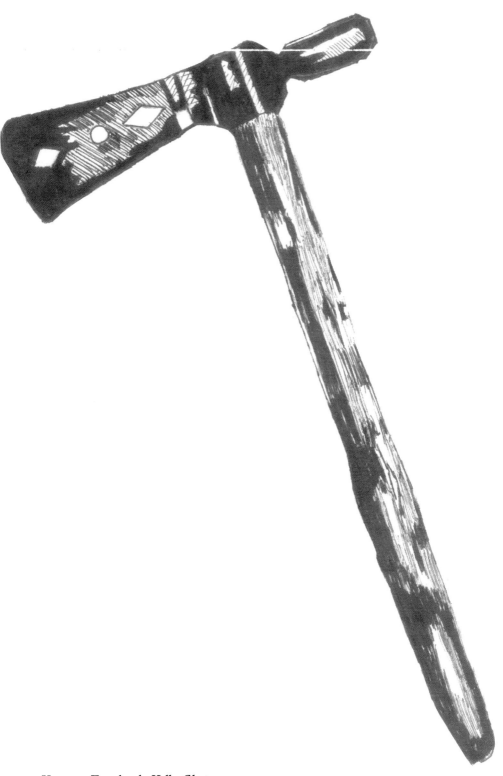

Yemassee Tomahawk. *Holley Gleaton.*

MURDER AND MAYHEM IN THE HOLY CITY

among the Native Americans. During his first year on the job, he accused the son-in-law of Governor Johnson of enslaving friendly Cherokees and stealing their deerskins. His tough and fair treatment of the Native Americans earned him a brief stint in jail on a false charge of treason. If anyone could forestall hostilities with the Yamassee, it was Nairne.

On April 14, 1715, Nairne and a delegation comprising experienced frontiersmen William Bray, Samuel Warner, John Cochran and John Wright, arrived at the Yamassee village at Pocotaligo. The day was rife with tense negotiations but Nairne's honest approach seemed to win the day. With everything now seemingly resolved, the men were treated to a large meal and "passed the night in seeming friendship and tranquility." At the break of dawn they were awakened by the bloodcurdling war cries of the Yamassee warriors. They were quickly seized by men covered in the black and red war paint that one survivor said made the Yamassee look like "devils coming out of Hell."

William Bray, Samuel Warner and John Wright were quickly killed with hammers and hatchets. John Cochran and his wife were held briefly but they too were murdered. For Nairne a more terrible death was reserved. He was strapped down by the Yamassee and his skin was pierced with resinous pine splinters that were then set afire. His screams, as the flaming splinters passed into his body, were heard for four days until he mercifully died. Only two white men would survive that day at Pocotaligo. One man had wandered off during the night and fallen asleep in the woods. When he heard the commotion at daybreak, he slipped off into the marsh where he witnessed the massacre of his friends. Captain Seymore made a break for it the moment he awoke and fought his way out of the crowd of Indians. In the process, he was shot twice: the first shot hit him the back; the second shot crashed into his face, taking many of his teeth when it exited. Despite his horrific injuries, Seymore fled through the woods and "by swimming one mile and running ten" he reached John Barnwell's plantation where he alerted the neighborhood to the coming attack. The warning provided time enough to evacuate Beaufort's three hundred inhabitants to the safety of a merchant ship lying in the harbor. From the deck of that ship, the settlers watched the Yamassee enter Beaufort and burn their homes to the ground.

As one war party burned Beaufort, another group of Yamassee attacked the frontier plantations, "spreading desolation and slaughter." The English were totally unprepared, and their attackers torched plantation houses, fields, barns and anything else that belonged to, or served, the whites. By nightfall, nearly a hundred settlers had been killed between the Combahee and Stono Rivers. From the walls of Charles Town, the colonists could see the light of the burning plantations. The inferno is said to have burned almost continuously for several days.

Considering that only one hundred colonists were killed that first day, it is obvious that many fled into the woods to make their way alone to Charles Town over the next few days. Though some were killed en route, a few made it, the images of unmitigated slaughter indelibly stamped upon their minds. Charles Town erupted into fear as these survivors arrived at the city gates. To the residents of Charles Town, it was easy to visualize nearly the entire colony being slaughtered, much like what had happened at Jamestown, Virginia. How could it be otherwise? Nine thousand armed, frenzied warriors falling upon the defenseless, panicked city (including women and children). It was certainly easy to imagine.

With the Yamassee advancing, the colonists thought it most advisable to become the assailant without delay, and a considerable force was raised to fight the Native Americans. As hostile Indians gathered on all sides, a proposed march of the militia to meet the Yamassee was postponed, as soldiers threw up a fort on the Ashepoo River. They lingered. Tensions mounted.

As the sun came up, the militia attacked on two fronts. Governor Craven's detachment found the Yamassee exiting the Salkehatchie Swamp near the Combahee River. The Indians quickly surrounded the colonists and, for a time, it looked like all was lost. The Yamassee began to retreat at length when several of their chiefs were shot and killed. The retreat speedily became a rout and the surviving Yamassee warriors disappeared into the trees. The carnage was enormous. Many Europeans had been slain but the destruction of the Yamassee was worse. The fire from the muskets had blasted apart faces, limbs and torsos. Unlike the arrow and hatchet, whose wounds the Native Americans could treat, when a musket ball hit flesh, it expanded, spilling intestines, crushing bone and leaving gaping holes. It must have been a sad and macabre scene to look out over a field of horribly disfigured and dismembered corpses. The precedent was set: the war would be without truce or mercy.

While this battle was concluding, Captain Alexander MacKay and Colonel John Barnwell slipped up behind the Yamassee town of

Pocotaligo and scattered the few remaining defenders. They then proceeded to a nearby fort defended by two hundred Yamassee warriors. Though outnumbered, the militia stormed the fort and the celebrated Indian fighter John Palmer leapt the wall and killed several warriors. Despite their ferocity, the Native Americans fell in large numbers to the colonists' firepower and were forced to withdraw. The English were waiting in ambush and they unleashed a murderous volley of musket fire as the warriors came into the open. Now with their swords unleashed, the cavalry charged the Yamassee as they ran for the forest, hacking off arms and heads. Only a few survived that onslaught as the horsemen mercilessly trampled and hewed the last pockets of disorganized fighters.

Just as Governor Craven was consolidating his victory in the south, word reached him that the Catawaba and Congaree Indians were approaching from the north, killing everyone as they advanced. The Santee area was totally unaware of the danger and suffered some of the highest death tolls of any neighborhood during the uprising. Once news of the attacks on the Santee plantations reached Charles Town, "ninety horsemen" under the command of Captain Barker rode out to meet them. The colonists were ambushed only a few miles outside of town and Barker was among those killed. At this point only sixteen miles stood between Charles Town and total destruction.

It was undoubtedly a scene of utter pandemonium and terror, but many of the planters had organized and were preparing for another counterattack. With every home threatened, every able-bodied man turned out to fight. Captain George Chicken's company of seventy planters and forty slaves struck out to fight nearly four hundred Catawaba warriors and their allies. It was a dangerous undertaking. Just beyond the city walls, the wide extent of country might very possibly contain thousands of warriors spoiling for a fight. The battle for Charles Town commenced at Andrew Percival's fortified plantation called The Ponds. Captain Chicken accepted battle in a withdrawn defensive position and waited for the Native Americans to advance. The Catawba and Congaree were outgunned but they placed great confidence in their warriors, who outnumbered the colonists four to one. There came the horrible crash of musket fire and dying horses, and there they stood locked together in battle. As neither side would withdraw, the struggle was prolonged and bloody. Confusion steadily increased. At last, the Catawba and Congaree were hurled back with severe losses from the musket fire. The slaughter ended only in the depths of the woods, and the scattered Indians became fugitives—hunted, starving and suffering, but still in arms.

Though the colonists had halted the first wave of attacks, the Yamassee War swiftly transformed South Carolina into a broken colony on the verge of extinction. The colonists immediately dispatched emissaries to England and begged the Lords Proprietors for help, "representing to them the weak state of the province, the deplorable dangers which hung over it, and begging their paternal help and protection." With most of the colony now abandoned and Charles Town holding on by little more than a thread, the Proprietors thought any more expenditures on the colony would be a waste. They pledged nothing in defense of the colony in the midst of an increasingly anarchic situation. The colonists were on their own.

The settlers started to count their dead and it was thought that perhaps two hundred had been killed in the opening assault. And those were the lucky ones. Many colonists were burned alive or subjected to other unspeakable tortures. Others unhappily lived out short lives as slaves in the villages and forests of Florida, the prisoners of the Indians and their Spanish allies.

Though little has survived into the historic record, it is certain that these settlers witnessed the violent deaths of neighbors and loved ones before being abducted; that they endured the "hardships of hunger, sickness, and confinement" while they lived with their enemies, and that only a few were ever seen alive again. In her book *Charleston: The Place and People*, Mrs. St. Julien Ravenel told the story of one survivor:

> *Mrs. Burrows was taken by a "scalping party" and carried with her child to St. Augustine. The child cried and was instantly killed, and she was ordered under pain of death, not to weep for him! After being kept prisoner several years, she was allowed to return to Charles Town, where she told the Governor that the "Huspah King" who had captured her had told her that his orders from Spain were to kill every white man and bring every Negro alive to St. Augustine, and that rewards were given for such services.*

Though the English had driven the Yamassee and their allies away from Charleston, there was little doubt that they were reconstituting their forces for another assault. The Southern settlements were

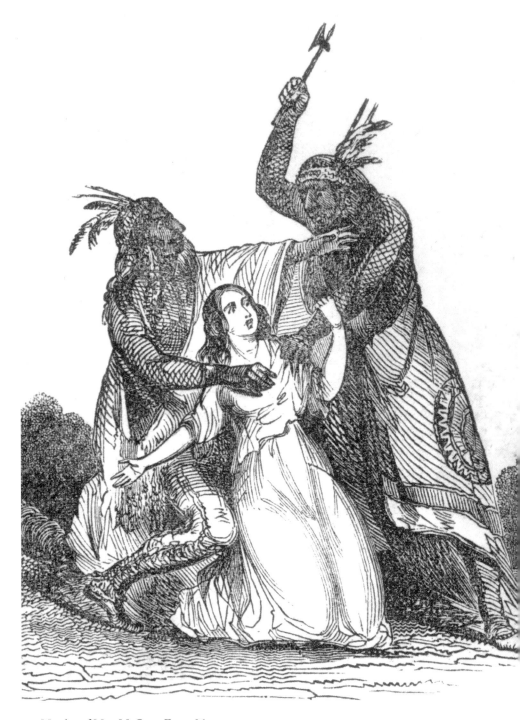

Murder of Mrs. McCrea. *Frost 1860*.

abandoned and the colonists constructed a ring of forts to hold Charles Town. Thereafter, the colonists could warily till their fields. The frontier fortifications were not a foolproof system, however, and the Yamassee frequently penetrated the perimeter and wreaked havoc on the settlements. The worst disaster happened after a hard night of drinking when the militia at Schinkin permitted the entry of a Native American scout supposedly allied to the English.

> *As soon as all were asleep he opened the gate for the entrance for his comrades. All the white men were murdered, many while still asleep; only one Negro boy leapt the stockade, and running through the woods all the Wantoot gave the alarm. Major Hyrne, commanding the garrison there, immediately marched to Schinkins and finding the Indians in turn overcome with liquor, put them all to the sword.*

As the fighting grew into a full-scale war, it appeared that the tribal confederation's overwhelming numerical superiority would end in Charles Town's complete destruction. This would have been a virtual certainty if the confederacy had successfully drawn the Cherokee into their cause. Instead, the Cherokee allied themselves with the Carolinians, and launched a fierce attack on the Yamassee's western flank. In a further stroke of good fortune, the besieged settlers received reinforcements from North Carolina and weapons from New England—a fortuitous event not guaranteed in an age of intense colonial rivalries.

By 1720, the conflict settled into a deadly war of attrition. Both sides massacred indiscriminately, and terrible cruelties were perpetrated to take possession of the land. With the Cherokee now allied with the English, the outcome of the war could be predicted with a grim mathematical certainty. But the Yamassee continued to appear on the Carolina frontier, killing and spreading terror throughout the colony. One contemporary recalled the barbarity during the second phase of the conflict:

> *[T]he Yamassee Indians...harboured in their breasts the most inveterate ill-will and rancour to all Carolineans, and watched every opportunity of pouring their vengeance on them. Being furnished with arms and ammunition from the Spaniards, they often broke out on small scalping parties, and infested the frontiers*

of the British settlement. One party of them catched William Hooper, and killed him by degrees, by cutting off one joint of his body after another, until he expired. Another party surprised Henry Quinton, Thomas Simmons, and Thomas Parmenter, and, to gratify their revenge, tortured them to death. Dr. Rose afterwards fell also into their hands, whom they cut across his nose with their tomahawk, and having scalped him left him on the spot for dead; but he happily recovered of his wounds. In short, the emissaries of St. Augustine, disappointed in their sanguinary design of destroying root and branch in Carolina, had now no other resource left but to employ the vindictive spirit of the Yamassees against the defenceless frontiers of the province. In these excursions, it must be confessed, they were too successful, for many poor settlers at different times fell a sacrifice to their insatiable revenge.

The colonists especially dreaded the prospect of scalping. A soldier from the colonial period described how the act was executed:

As soon as the man is felled, they run up to him, thrust their knee in between his shoulder blades, seize a tuft of hair in one hand &, with their knife in the other, cut around the skin of the head & pull the whole piece away. The whole thing is done very expeditiously. Then, brandishing the scalp, they utter a whoop which they call the "death whoop"...If they are not under pressure & the victory has cost them lives, they behave in an extremely cruel manner towards those they kill or the dead bodies. They disembowel them & smear their blood all over themselves.

As the year pressed on, the tide slowly turned against the Yamassee. They were first pushed into Georgia then eventually moved to Florida. There, the tribe was virtually annihilated when the Creek Indians abandoned the confederacy and allied themselves with the English. While the Yamassee and their allies staged a number of successful raids to the south throughout the 1720s, by 1728 the colonists had routed them and made the area accessible for renewed settlement.

Thereafter, the Yamassee practically vanished. Most were absorbed by the Lower Creeks and formed the Seminole tribe, a name meaning "wild people" or "runaway." They remained a tough bunch. Hiding in the farthest reaches of the Everglades, the Seminole held out against a relentless series of assaults from the United States military until the nineteenth century.

Victory in the Yamassee War saved the colony, but success came at a high price. The war had reduced the colony to a shadow of its former self and transformed South Carolina into an even crueler and more violent place than before. The war also intensified the animosity toward all Native Americans and the removal of the Yamassee from South Carolina was followed by a war of extermination against or emigration of nearly every tribe in the vicinity of Charles Town. Hunted from place to place, and disheartened by continual abuses, the Native Americans had totally abandoned the Lowcountry by the mid-eighteenth century. Manifest Destiny had begun.

THE LEGEND
OF LAVINIA AND
THE SIX MILE HOUSE

I f Lavinia Fisher was as captivating in life as she is in death, it is no wonder her gang made such a successful run of tricking unsuspecting travelers and weary wagon traders out of their property. Even before she ever set foot to the gallows, Lavinia's legend began, as she was plucked from Backcountry obscurity to fill the role of beautiful outlaw and dangerous murderess. Lavinia cast a spell over Charleston that has held residents and visitors alike in thrall for almost two hundred years.

No one knows for sure where Lavinia's story begins, where she was from, who was her kin or what circumstances would have compelled her to marry John Fisher and join a gang of thieves. By all accounts, she seized upon this lifestyle with great enthusiasm, her skills in scheming and cruelty perhaps even surpassing her husband's. The enormity of Lavinia's legend is extraordinary given that all that we know of her today comes from a handful of personal accounts and official papers documenting her exploits over little more than a year. Though none of the accounts passed down through the generations consistently describe even the color of her hair, they do agree that she was a strikingly beautiful woman with a shockingly crude vocabulary.

There are as many variations of Lavinia's story as there are people who tell it, but the most popular version typically goes something like this:

Lavinia and John Fisher ran a modest but well-kept inn on a lonely stretch of road in Charleston. The inn's warmly lit windows were a welcome sight to many weary travelers, though it was rumored that some of the guests who checked in never checked out. One night, a fur trader named John Peoples was passing by and he decided to stop for the night; it was late and the weather was poor. Upon entering, the trader was greeted by the innkeeper's beautiful wife, Lavinia. He found her to be very friendly, perhaps too friendly, for the simple trader soon became suspicious of the Fishers' intentions and politely refused the refreshments they offered, fearing they were poisoned, and retired to bed early.

As the night wore on, the trader's uneasiness grew and he found it difficult to sleep. He decided not to stay in the bed, resting instead in a corner of the room in case someone should enter in the middle of the night to assault him. His suspicions were eventually confirmed when the bed fell through a trap door into the cellar where John Fisher waited with an axe. At once the trader escaped and returned to Charleston to report the incident to the authorities there. John and Lavinia were subsequently arrested, and a search of the property revealed a great number of human remains, many found in a pit of lime in the cellar beneath the trap door.

John and Lavinia Fisher were condemned to die. On the day of the execution, John Fisher was hanged first. His last words were wasted on meek pleas for his life and laying blame on his wife for their crimes. Lavinia, standing on the platform in her wedding gown, kissed her dead husband, then turned to address the crowd. "If you have a message you want to send to hell, give it to me," she said, "I'll carry it!" The silence of the crowd was only broken by the crack of her neck as she finally met her end. It is said that Lavinia's presence is still strongly felt at the Old Jail on Magazine Street, where she was imprisoned for a year before her hanging, and in the Unitarian Church graveyard where she was buried.

Some people say Lavinia Fisher was the first woman hanged in America, but in fact that distinction belongs to Margaret Hatch who was hanged in Virginia in 1633 for murder. Some also say that Lavinia and her husband were South Carolina's most notorious serial killers, though Pee Wee Gaskins more honestly fits this role. In truth, the fiction has very little in common with the fact. The fact is that John and Lavinia did not run an inn, they did not act alone, the remains of no more than two bodies were ever officially reported to have been found and the Fishers were never charged with or convicted of murder. There was, however, a trader named John Peoples who reported an incident involving John and Lavinia to the authorities, and it was this incident that ultimately led to their arrest, though not for murder. The entire episode happened out of doors, and Peoples certainly didn't find Lavinia overly friendly—or friendly at all.

The wagon trade was a successful industry in Charleston, but in 1819 it began to suffer at the hands of an outlaw gang in the Backcountry that made a living relieving wagon traders of their hard-earned money and goods. The wagon traders started traveling with their rifles at the ready, or simply stopped trading in Charleston altogether. Because none of the victims had been able to identify their assailants, the authorities' hands were tied. Unwilling to watch the profitable wagon trade die, a cavalcade of citizens rode into Charleston's Backcountry in an exercise of "Lynch's Law" to put an end to the gang's activities. According to the February 19 *News and Courier*,

> *A gang of desperadoes have for some time past occupied certain houses, and infested the road leading to this city, in the vicinity of Ashley Ferry; practising every deception upon the unwary, and frequently committing robberies upon defenceless travelers. As they could not be identified, and thereby brought to punishment, it was determined, by a number of citizens, to break them up, and they accordingly proceeded, in a cavalcade, on Thursday afternoon, to the spot, having previously obtained permission of the owners of some small houses, to which these desperadoes resorted, to proceed against the premises in such manner as circumstances might require.*

The cavalcade's destinations were the Five and Six Mile Houses, reputed to be the gang's favored haunts. At the Five Mile House, the occupants were given fifteen minutes to vacate the premises before it was burned to the ground. The citizens then proceeded to the Six Mile House, the Fishers' "well-kept inn" of legend, where they evicted the occupants without a fight and left a young man by the name of David Ross to guard the property. Believing the matter had been put to an end, the cavalcade returned triumphant to Charleston. Early the next morning, however, two men from the gang, one later identified as William Hayward, broke into the house and assaulted Dave Ross, pushing him outside. When Ross looked up, he found that he was surrounded by the other members of the gang. Among those surrounding him was Lavinia Fisher. He had admired her beauty when he saw her in town, and now he looked to her for help. Instead of the gentle response Ross must have been expecting, Lavinia reached down and choked him, and shoved his head through a window. Stunned and beaten, Ross somehow managed to escape his captors, disappearing into the woods before making his way to the authorities.

Two hours later, John Peoples was heading out of town in his wagon when he stopped near the Six Mile House to water his horses. A man came out of the house and approached the wagon, asking Peoples's traveling companion for his bucket. When the request was refused, the man flew into a rage, and nine or ten men and a woman brandishing clubs, guns and pistols came out of the house and beat Peoples. He would later testify that a woman beat him over the head and eyes with a stick. Just as suddenly as the attack had begun, it ended, and the gang reentered the house. Peoples got back into his wagon and made haste on the road home, but he had covered less than two hundred yards when two members of the gang reappeared, drawing guns and stealing about forty dollars. This time, Peoples decided to return to Charleston to alert the authorities, and this time, the victim had gotten a good look at the members of the gang. He told authorities that he did not know the names of all of the people in the gang, but he had "just cause to believe that among them was William Hayward, John Fisher and his Wife Lavinia Fisher, Joseph Roberts and John Andrews."

This report, closely following Ross's claims, forced the law into action. Judge Charles Jones Colcock issued a bench warrant, and the sheriff's deputy, Colonel Nathaniel Green Cleary, set out for the Six Mile House. When he arrived, he found John and Lavinia Fisher, Seth Young and Jane Howard. Rather than expose his wife to the dangers of gunfire, John surrendered the group. They were taken to the jail on Magazine Street

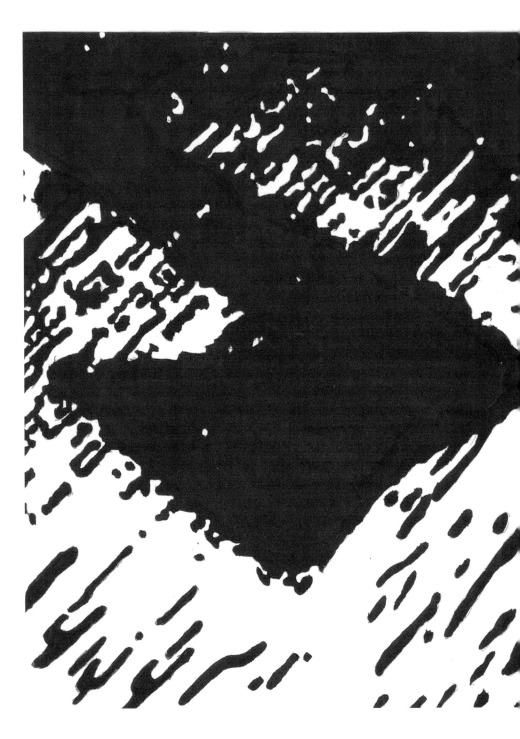

John Fisher's axe. *Andrew Richardson*.

where they were joined by William Hayward. They would be reunited with still other members of the gang as they were rounded up over the next few days and sent to Magazine Street.

The prisoners were brought, one at a time, before Cleary and a group of twenty or thirty citizens. Peoples identified the group as the people who attacked him. The Fishers were jailed on suspicion of highway robbery—a hanging offense at that time. While the Fishers awaited a hearing, a grave containing the remains of two people was uncovered two hundred yards from the ashes of the Six Mile House. The remains were believed to be those of a white male and a black female, and were estimated to have been there for at least two years. This grave represents all of the remains that were reported discovered in the vicinity of the Six Mile House. With any number of people squatting in this den of iniquity, it would have been quite difficult to identify those specifically responsible for the deaths. As such, no one was charged or tried for these murders.

After a month in prison, the Fishers, Hayward and Roberts were brought before a judge for a hearing. Hayward and Roberts were let out on bail, but the Fishers were sent back to jail to await trial at the next session. The defendants pled not guilty when the case was heard in May, but their fellow citizens disagreed—the Fishers were found guilty of highway robbery. When they appeared before Judge Colcock for sentencing, their lawyer presented a motion to appeal the case at the Constitutional Court. The judge made no objection, and so the Fishers were granted a reprieve until the court met again in January.

John and Lavinia kept themselves busy over the next eight months planning their escape. On account of the fact that Lavinia was a lovely woman, and she and John were married, they had been moved from the bowels of the jail to the debtors' quarters in one of the upper stories. One of their neighbors was fellow gang member Joseph Roberts, who had made bail at the same hearing that sent the Fishers to trial. Soon after making bail, Roberts was picked up again, this time charged with threatening the life of a butcher. He tried to flee the scene on horseback, but broke his horse's neck jumping a ditch on Queen Street and was hauled back to jail.

Looking out the windows day after day, the prisoners' escape route soon became clear. They were not under strict surveillance in their new quarters, so on Monday, September 13, they were able to make a hole under a window and use a rope made of blankets to let themselves to the ground. Lavinia was last in line, but as John made his way, the rope snapped and he dropped to the ground. He was not hurt, but Lavinia was trapped inside with no way out. Their plan had been to board a ship bound for Cuba, but John would not leave without Lavinia.

Fisher and Roberts were recaptured the next night when a storekeeper recognized them. They were sent back to jail where they were heavily guarded. No other opportunity for escape would present itself. Worse, the Fishers' motion for a new hearing was rejected by the Constitutional Court. The Fishers had run out of options. They were sentenced to hang on February 4, and only word from the governor could save them. Lavinia's cause was taken up by Charleston's finest ladies, who implored Governor John Geddes not to execute a woman, but to no avail. The governor did not save the Fishers, but he did give them a brief respite of two weeks so that they could have "an opportunity for repentance" and "time to meet their God." This extra time only prolonged Lavinia's suffering, waiting as she did every waking moment, expecting a full pardon with every footstep that approached her cell and cursing at every disappointment.

The Reverend Richard Furman visited the Fishers every day to help them prepare to meet their maker. By all accounts Furman did make progress with John, though it is doubtful Lavinia was fully prepared to meet her God. Her prayers continued to devolve into curses as her day drew near.

The gallows were erected on Meeting Street, just beyond the Charleston city lines. Executions were events for the masses, but the sensational aspects of this particular execution also brought out Charleston's fine ladies who came to witness the end of lovely Lavinia. The Fishers, wearing loose white robes over their clothes, were transported to the gallows in a coach with Reverend Furman and the hangman. When they arrived, Lavinia could not be persuaded to mount the scaffold. The constables eventually had to drag her up the stand where she beseeched the crowd, arms outstretched, to rescue her. According to one historian's account, "She stamped in rage and swore with all the vehemence of her amazing vocabulary, calling down damnation on a governor who would let a woman swing. The crowd stood shocked into silence, while she cut short one oath with another and ended with a volley of shrieks."

Once Lavinia had been calmed down, Reverend Furman read a letter written by John Fisher the morning of his execution:

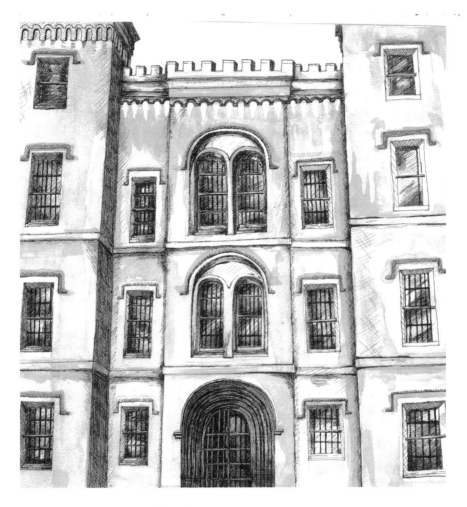

The Old Charleston jail. *Nick Hendrix.*

Reverend and Dear Sir,
The appointed day has arrived—the moment soon to come, which will finish my earthly career; and it behoves me, for the last time, to address you and the reverend gentlemen associated in your pious care.
For your exertions in explaining the mysteries of our Holy Religion and the merits of our dear Redeemer: for pious sympathy, and benevolent regards as concerns our immortal souls, accept Sir, for yourself, and them, the last benediction of the unfortunate – God, in his infinite mercy reward you all.

In a few moments, and the world to me shall have passed away—before the Throne of the Eternal Majesty of Heaven I must stand—shall then, at this dreadful hour, my convulsed, agitated lips, still proclaim a falsehood? No! then by that Awful Majesty I swear, I am innocent. May the Redeemer of the World plead for those who have sworn away my life.

To the unfortunate, the voice of condolence is sweet-the language of commiseration delightful—these feelings I have experienced in the society of Mr. ——.

A stranger, he rejected not our prayer; unknown, he shut not his ear to our supplication; he has alleviated our sorrows—May God bless him. He has wept with us—May Angels rejoice with him at a throne of glory.

Enclosed, Sir, is a key that secretes my little all—Give it to him, and say for me, as he deserted me not while living, I hope he will discharge my last request. How my property is to be disposed of, he will find explained in a paper within my trunk, to which is attached a Schedule of the whole. I only wish him to see it removed to a place of safety, until to whom it is given shall call for it. The hour is come!

Farewell, Sir, Farewell!

John Fisher

As Reverend Furman drew silent, Fisher proclaimed his innocence. Addressing the crowd, Fisher stated, "Colonel Cleary called me and the other prisoners in jail by name to Peoples so as to enable him to identify me and the others—and my blood is on Colonel Cleary's hands." Finally he asked for forgiveness from the crowd and turned to Lavinia, who was looking to the sheriff until the very end awaiting news of a pardon. None forthcoming, the ropes were made, the knots were tied and the caps placed over the prisoners' heads. The sheriff gave the signal and the platform fell. Perhaps Lavinia had bewitched the hangman as well, for she died quickly, but poor John kicked for several minutes.

If Lavinia's legend hadn't already begun, her last words would surely have sealed the deal. They were, indeed, "If you have a message you want to send to hell, give it to me—I'll carry it."

THE FANATICISM OF
THE FAMILY DUTARTRE

The creation of the Charles Towne settlement coincided with a time of intense religious upheavals in European society. When Louis XIV became king of France, he revoked the Edict of Nantes, and four hundred thousand French Protestants, called Huguenots, were forced to abandon their homes. Thus it happened that a considerable number of South Carolina's early settlers were French Huguenots who sought the prospect of securing religious liberty.

The Huguenots were the backbone of France: artisans, mechanics and professionals of all sorts. According to one early historian of the colony:

> At this period these new settlers were a great acquisition to Carolina. They had taken the oath of allegiance to the king, and promised fidelity to the Proprietors. They were disposed to look on the settlers, whom they had joined, in the favorable light of bretheren and fellow adventurers, and though they understood not the English language, yet they were desirous of living in peace and harmony with their neighbors, and willing to stand forth on all occasions of danger with them for the common safety and defense.

Though a few of the Huguenots settled on the Charles Towne peninsula, most families settled in an area of St. Dennis Parish called the Orange Quarter. On the banks of French Quarter Creek, they founded their church and built their homes. Desiring a place of their own to preserve the French language, many families immigrated to the Santee River neighborhood where they farmed their land and increased their properties. After worshipping in French as a separate congregation, many eventually intermarried with the British settlers and became members of the Church of England.

As the Huguenots along the Santee prospered and became among the most powerful families in the colony, it proved to be difficult in Charles Towne for the Dutartres. Among the first Huguenots to arrive in Carolina, by their second generation, the Dutartres, now grown to include four sons, four daughters and several spouses, were living in a ramshackle house outside of town. The men worked as farmers, carpenters and sawyers, while the women and children worked in the house and fields. Regardless of age or sex, they all grew, tended and harvested the food they ate, just as they spun the thread and wove they clothes wore. It was a tough living, but the family was self-sufficient and in some ways better off than their neighbors, who were often harassed by creditors. Their hard work did not go unnoticed by their neighbors, who claimed the family "always maintained an honest character, and were...of blameless and irreproachable lives."

As with their fellow countrymen in the Orange Quarter, the Dutartre family had encountered extenuating circumstances that made them willing to combat unknown hardships in their search for freedom, a new home and happiness. Freedom of worship was perhaps the prime reason for the family's move to America. The father was a zealous and rigid Calvinist, inheriting an almost constitutional hatred of Catholicism as a result of the persecutions by which he had suffered so much and so long. The mother was no less zealous in her views, descended as she was from the same background of religious discrimination. The Dutartres weren't sure their Anglican neighbors were much of an improvement over their previous circumstances. The English elites were altogether obsessed with material things and the Dutartres were deeply suspicious of Charles Town, a "wicked" place—a place caught up in violence and the relentless pursuit of wealth.

Estranged from the larger culture, the Dutartres turned to their faith to seek comfort and make sense of their world. It was a time when spiritual enthusiasms were bubbling over in South Carolina and people believed the apocalypse was at hand. In these confusing times, the demarcation between superstition and religion was not always clear, and the colony was crawling with mystics hawking their visions. Around 1722, the Dutartres were introduced to a traveling prophet. He was a mysterious presence who found an audience for his "illiterate enthusiasm and wild imagination" at the Dutartres home. His influence steadily grew and he "filled their Heads with many wild and fantastic Notions," as Anglican Commissary Alexander Garden later told it. Although in one account Garden identified this preacher as Christian George, it was very likely Michael Wolfhart, a traveling prophet from Pennsylvania who took a missionary journey to South Carolina in 1722.

Wolfhart was spreading the word of Jacob Boehme, a German religious mystic from the town of Goerlitz on the Polish side of the Oder River. A cobbler by profession, Boehme had a seminal religious epiphany in 1600, when a ray of sunlight reflected in a pewter dish catapulted him into an ecstatic vision of God penetrating all existence. After his first revelation, he continued to have mystical experiences and wrote about them in a series of obscure religious treatises. According to Boehme, negativity and suffering are essential aspects of the deity, for it is only through the participating in man's suffering that God achieves full self-consciousness of his own nature. For whatever reason, the teachings resonated with the Dutartre family and they invited Wolfhart to live in their home. Their teacher came and went, but

> *unhappily for the poor family those strange notions gained ground on them, insomuch that in one year they began to withdraw themselves from the ordinances of public worship, and all conversation with the world around them, and strongly to imagine they were the only family upon earth who had the knowledge of the true God, and whom he vouchsafed to instruct, either by the immediate impulses of his Spirit, or by signs and tokens from heaven.*

The Dutartres became everyday more withdrawn from the community and that generated a robust flow of gossip. Though the family was certainly aware of the growing scandal, their neighbors' mockery was irrelevant. In their mind, Charles Town's residents were too ignorant and corrupt to grasp God's plan for the family. It was about this time that one of their own began to prophesy. The prophet was Peter Rombert, second husband of the family's eldest daughter who had remarried when she was widowed. Through a series of revelations, he announced God's intentions to destroy the world save for "one Family, whom he would preserve as he did Noah's, for raising up a Godly Seed again upon it."

When Rombert told the Dutartres of his revelations, they were at first skeptical but he persisted, explaining that the apocalypse was at hand and that the Dutartres were God's chosen people. They were commanded to accept this responsibility without question. Refusal would result in their eternal damnation. When Rombert revealed God's order to prepare for the imminent cataclysm, the family's skepticism turned a little more toward belief. They had reason to think there would be trouble. Many of the Huguenots situated along the Santee River had been slaughtered in 1715 by a Catawaba war party, and deaths by ambush on lonely plantations were not uncommon. It was a time of great alarm throughout the colony as the Native Americans and their Spanish allies threatened to push Charles Town into the sea. Everything seemed to confirm that South Carolina was teetering precariously close to destruction, just as Rombert had prophesied.

Rombert's prophecies continued to revolve around the Dutartre family:

> *God was pleased to reveal himself a second time to the prophet, saying, Put away the woman whom thou hast for thy wife, and when I have destroyed this wicked generation, I will raise up her first husband from the dead, and they shall be man and wife as before, and go thou and take to wife her youngest sister, who is a virgin, so shall the chosen family be restored entire, and the holy seed preserved pure and undefiled in it. At first the father, when he heard of this revelation, was staggered at so extraordinary a command from heaven; but the prophet assured him that God would give him a sign, which accordingly happened; upon which the old man took his youngest daughter by the hand, and gave her to the wise prophet immediately for his wife, who without further ceremony took the damsel and deflowered her. Thus for some time they continued in acts of incest and adultery, until that period which made the fatal discovery, and introduced the bloody scene of blind fanaticism and madness.*

Rombert's next commandment for the family, as revealed to him by God, was even more staggering: the prophet was to plant his seed with

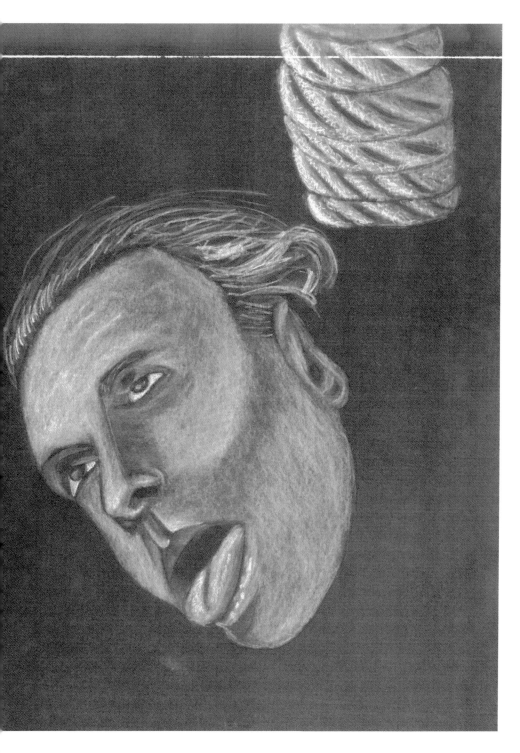

The hanging of the Dutartres. *Nick Hendrix.*

each of the Dutartres women. If he failed to impregnate them, the men of the family should use incest to fulfill their ordained mission as the next Adam and Eve. They were assured that it was God's command and that it would not be sin for father to be with daughter, brother with sister or mother with son.

The Dutartres readily accepted Rombert's prophecy, blind to the effect their arrangement was beginning to have on the community. In a place as small as Charles Town, this sort of behavior did not go unnoticed, and indignant neighbors resolved to stamp out such acts of depravity in their midst. The situation was further inflamed when Rombert asserted that the family was no longer to obey the laws of the colony. For them, the laws of God took precedence over the laws of man. Some of their neighbors may have been able to overlook their failure to muster for the militia or fix local roads, but when it was revealed that the youngest child, Judith Dutartre, was pregnant, a "warrant was issued for bringing her before the Justice to be examined, and bound over to the general sessions, in consequence of a law of the province, framed for preventing bastardy."

Rombert knew from the beginning that his prophecy would draw the family into conflict with the Charles Town authorities, an incident for which he'd been preparing for the better part of a year. He'd been stockpiling weapons and instructing the family to construct a massive wall to encircle the plantation. The wall was ten feet high and, when defended with muskets, would have proved a formidable obstacle to even the most determined attack.

While the Dutartres awaited the arrival of the magistrate, Rombert did his best to inflame the situation, playing on the family's carefully cultivated sense of persecution. They were reminded again and again that God had chosen them alone and that they were above man's law. If, somehow, the authorities managed to enter their sanctuary, Rombert asserted that "God commanded them to arm and defend themselves against persecution, and their substance against the robberies of ungodly men; assuring them at the same time that no weapon formed against them should prosper."

Two days later, six men of the Charles Town militia, led by Captain Simmons, attempted to serve the warrant. Several of the Dutartres working in the fields spotted the men coming up the plantation road and, laying hold of their arms, fired on the constable and his followers. The magistrate, realizing that his lightly armed men had no chance of overtaking the armed house, made a hasty retreat.

Outraged, the militia gathered and began preparations to take the Dutartre home by force. Rombert urged the family to resist arrest and persuaded them that they were impervious to the bullets of "the Men of the Earth." The family, thinking themselves immune to musket fire, hunkered down and waited for the militia, aiming their guns at the approaching men. The first shot dropped Simmons, killing him instantly. Several other militiamen were wounded but managed to get out of the line of fire and take cover. They responded by unleashing a hail of gunfire into the home. The house was a simple timber frame affair and there was nowhere to hide. Within a few minutes, the militia had "killed one woman within the house, and afterwards forcibly entering it, took the rest prisoners, six in number, and brought them to Charlestown."

Charles Town was overtaken with grief when news reached town that Captain Simmons had been killed. Anguish soon became anger, and it was a minor miracle that the family wasn't lynched. This explosive atmosphere greeted the Dutartre family when they were brought to trial in September 1724. Facing certain death, they remained totally unrepentant and "confidently persisted in their Delusion till their last Breath," Reverend Garden, the Episcopal minister of Charles Town, noted. "They had obeyed the Voice of God, and were about to suffer Martyrdom for it." The people of Charles Town were more than happy to fulfill the family's death wish. Five were brought to trial, found guilty and condemned to die.

One contemporary probably captured the city's mood when he wrote the following passage:

> *Alas! Miserable creatures, what amazing infatuation possessed them! They pretended they had the Spirit of God leading them to all truth, they knew it and felt it: but this spirit, instead of influencing them to obedience, purity and peace, commanded them to commit rebellion, incest, and murder. What is still more astonishing, the principal persons among them, I mean the prophet, the father of the family, and Michel Boneau, never were convinced of their delusion, but persisted in it until their last breath. During their trial they appeared altogether unconcerned and secure, affirming that God was on their side, and therefore they feared not what man could do unto them. They freely told the incestuous story in open court in all its circumstances and aggravations, with a good countenance, and very readily confessed the facts respecting their rebellion and*

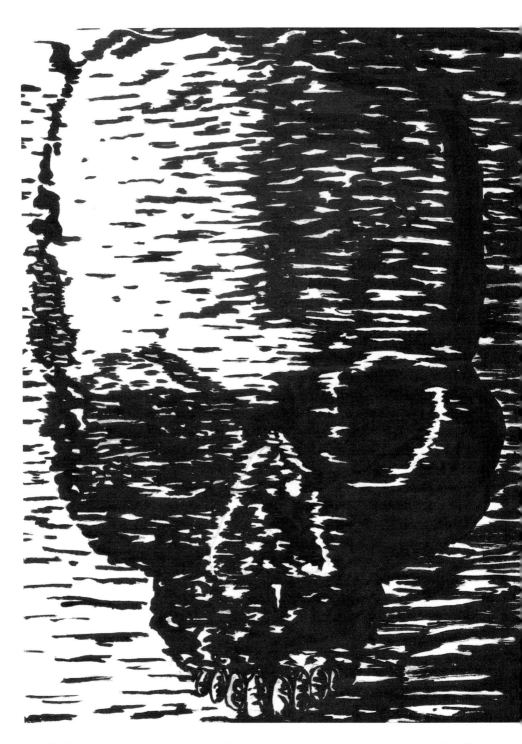

"God had assured them, that he would...raise them up from the dead on the third day."
Andrew Richardson.

murder, with which they stood charged, but pled their authority
from God in vindication of themselves, and insisted they had done
nothing in either case but by his express command.

Their fate decided, the Dutartres were housed in the Charles Town prison
to await hanging. As was commonly the practice, Alexander Garden began
to meet with the family "both to convince them of their error and danger,
and prepare them for death by bringing them to a penitent disposition."
The family dismissed Garden and responded that they had "obeyed the
voice of God, and were now about to suffer martyrdom for their religion.
But God had assured them, that he would either work a deliverance for
them, or raise them up from the dead on the third day." Three of the men
could not be shaken from this belief and at their execution they "told the
spectators with seeming triumph, they should soon see them again, for
they were certain they should rise from the dead on the third day." The
authorities had no such illusions and the men's bodies were left hanging
until the three days had come and gone.

With respect to the other three, the daughter Judith, being
with child, was not tried. The two sons, David and John Dutartre,
about eighteen and twenty years of age, having been also tried and
condemned, "continued sullen and reserved, in hopes of seeing those
that were executed rise from the dead but being disappointed, they
became, or at least seemed to become, sensible of their error." As
time wore on, public opinion began to turn in the brothers' favor,
and the execution was called off. They were released from prison, but
unfortunately, not long after, one of the brothers relapsed into his old
ways and "murdered an innocent person, without either provocation
or previous quarrel, and for no other reason, as he confessed, but that
God had commanded him so to do." Being brought to trial for a second
time, he was found guilty of murder and condemned. As he waited for
the day of execution, the young man was again visited by Minister
Garden who explained the terms of pardon and salvation proposed in
the Gospel. The visit appears to have made an impression. As the boy
went to the gallows, Garden said that he was "deeply sensible of his
error and delusion...and seemed to die in the humble mercy, through
the all-sufficient merits of a Redeemer." Thus ended that tragic story
of the Dutartre family, in which seven persons lost their lives: one was
killed, two were murdered and four executed for the murders.

AFFAIRS OF HONOR

The law affords no remedy that can satisfy the feelings of a true man.
Elizabeth Jackson

On a fall afternoon in 1856, one of Charleston's most respected men lay mortally wounded in a clearing alongside the Washington Racecourse, shot on the "field of honor." The fatal duel between William Taber Jr. and Edward Magrath shocked no one in Charleston. Both were Charlestonians, well respected and distinguished in their professions, just as both were tough-minded partisans, not incapable of killing if they thought it necessary.

Although the duel originated in France, it was a reflection of British culture, imported to the New World by aristocrats who believed that a man could neither ignore an insult nor back down from a fight. By the late colonial period, killing in the name of honor had become a well-established tradition in Charleston and its popularity would continue to grow for another hundred years.

In 1838, South Carolina Governor John Lyde Wilson codified dueling practices in a document called the *Code Duello*. The code contained twenty-five specific rules outlining all aspects of the duel, from how to load the weapons to the proper retraction required to end the affair.

One historian details how the duel was executed:

> *In a typical duel, each party acted through a second. The seconds'*
> *duty, above all, was to try to reconcile the parties without violence.*
> *An offended party sent a challenge through his second. If the*
> *recipient apologized, the matter usually ended. If he elected to*
> *fight, the recipient chose the weapons and the time and place of the*
> *encounter. Up until combat began, apologies could be given and the*
> *duel stopped. After combat began, it could be stopped at any point*
> *after honor had been satisfied.*

If dueling allegedly demonstrated the sincerity of a man's commitment to his honor, it also served as a way to assert one's superior qualities as a man. By professing the willingness to die for an ideal and by constantly testing others' willingness to do the same, the duelist sought public acclaim in a world where public acclaim was something everybody wanted.

Certainly Charleston's most important citizens subscribed to these ideals and many took up the practice of dueling with a passion. General William Moultrie met an unknown opponent in an alley near Philadelphia Street, and after a short fight, the general "succeeded in running his sword through his antagonists arm. He immediately withdrew it, wiped the blade, and after courteously saluting his antagonist turned the corner and attended divine services at St. Phillip's Church."

During a bitter political campaign in 1823, General John Geddes was challenged by Edward Simons. His son, Thomas Geddes, fought in his father's stead. The men fired four shots at one another, coming so close that their clothes were riddled with bullet holes. After each round, as the code provided, their seconds encouraged the combatants to mend their differences. Simons adamantly refused to sign a letter of apology. On the fifth round, Geddes was hit in the leg and Simons was shot dead. Judge J.F. Grimke narrowly averted death when Henry Laurens refused to shoot after the judge's pistol misfired. With Grimke cursing him to finish it, an exasperated Laurens tossed his pistol to the ground and rode off. Even President Andrew Jackson, born in the South Carolina Backcountry, learned that a challenge was a highly effective tool for silencing critics and repairing a damaged reputation. In 1806, Jackson shot a man after he was called a "worthless scoundrel...and a platoon and coward." A second gunfight nearly killed him but it also honed Jackson's fearful reputation and echoed his mother's sentiment that "The law affords no remedy that can satisfy the feelings of a true man."

The impetus for the duel may have been honor, but there were less noble reasons Charleston's wealthiest citizens killed one another. The fortunes of the Lowcountry plantations produced an excess of reckless young planters who had no ideals except to gamble and drink and ride, and whose only interest in life was violence and the glory they saw in it. Ralph Waldo Emerson said these men sprang forth from a culture in which man was "an animal, given to pleasure, frivolous, irritable, spending his days in hunting and practising with deadly weapons to defend himself against his slaves and against his companions brought up in the same idle and dangerous way."

The causes for a duel could be alarmingly simple. When diplomacy forestalled an argument over tax policy between Peter DeLancey and Dr. John Haly, the men could not let the disagreement die a natural death. An afternoon of drinking caused the argument to flare anew. A letter written to Ralph Izard details how the matter was finally resolved:

To Ralph Izard

Augt. 24th 1771.

Dr Sir

I am in Doubt whether you will be surprised either at the Death of DeLancey, or the Manner of it. I confess for my own Part, that it does not appear extraordinary to me that he should be killed in a Duel, & that by Dr. Haly. There was a Quarrel of several Years Standing between them, which always broke out afresh upon their being heated with Liquor. On Thursday the 15th Instant they dined together at Mr. Pendleton's, a Man you may remember by the Name of the Tall North Carolina Lawyer, & were observed to be much more sociable than usual. About 5 O Clock in the Afternoon the Landlord got drunk & was put to Bed, the Company which was numerous, then retired, all but Haly & Delancy who went together into the Balcony, & Charles Motte, who happened to be the last in the Room, & overheard them make an Appointment for Eight that Evening. They then parted, & DeLancey went home. His wife being abroad, he was obliged to break open a Door to get his Pistols, and being in want of Bullets, turned the Negroes out of the Kitchen, & cast them. About half an Hour after Seven, Several of us were at the Corner [Tavern], &

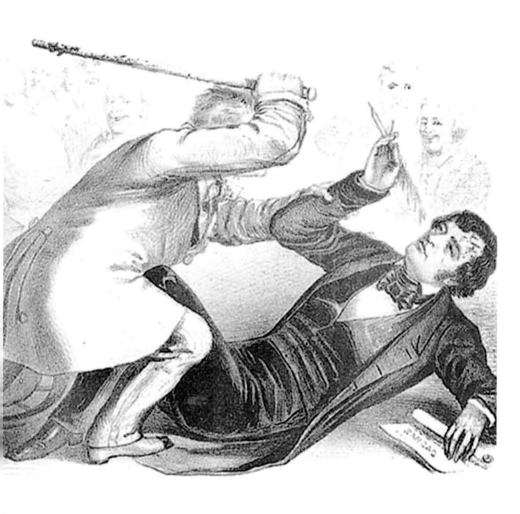

J.L. Magee cartoon of the Brooks-Sumner affair.

were joined by Charles Motte, Who in a Careless Way ment[ione]d that there was to have been an affair between Haly and DeLancey that evening at Seven, at Eight came Haly, staggering drunk, Upon which the Company took no Notice of the Matter, taking it for granted that if the Appointment was at Seven, the Affair must be over at Eight. But Motte had mistaken the Hour. Haly went off, & in a few minutes the Rest of the Company separated. In my Way home as I passed by the Holliday's Tavern at the Corner of Queen Street, I found a Mob was gathering & was told a Man had been killed in the House. Dr. Farquharson happened to be with me, & immediately stepped in, & upon his Return told me DeLancey was dead. They had met in a small Room at the Tavern, about 15 by 12 Feet. They called for a Bottle of Wine, & shut the Door. Immediately afterwards, two Pistols were heard to go off, so quick, that the Sound of each could just be distinguished. A Master of Vessel immediately called to them to open the Door. Haly answered he could not but desired him to break it open, which was done as fast as possible. Haly pushed out desiring they would take Care of the wounded Man, & DeLancey was found shot in the Breast with a single Bullet, about two Inches from the Right Pap & rather below it. He never spoke, & 'tis probable his Death was instantaneous. On the other Side of the Room two Pistol Bullets were found one in the Wainscot about 5 feet from the Floor, & the other in the Base, By this it should appear that DeLancey had fired with a Brace of Balls. They had exchanged Pistols. & it is thought had loaded in the Room, as Powder & Ball were found on the Table. Haly got off, But where he is at present is not known. DeLancey was buried the next Day at Eleven O Clock. The Intemperance of the weather, joined to the state of his body, overheated as he certainly was, with Liquor and Passions, caused so quick a Putrification that it was absolutely necessary to bury him so soon. I have given you an exact Account of this unhappy Affair. The Consequences of which had like to have been fatal to the poor little Woman. But I am happy to tell you that she is at length better resigned to her Misfortune. I make no Reflections upon the matter, to you they would be needless. It is enough that you have a true Relation of this Transaction in which no body suspects any foul Play, as far as it has come to the knowledge of &ca

R. Izard

Bound by something more powerful than honor, religious leaders and newspaper editors worked hard to stop duels. But denunciations such as Reverend Weems's illustrated pamphlet "God's Revenge Against Dueling" did little to move public sentiment. After the deaths of two young planters in the fall of 1807, the *Charleston City Gazette* joined the condemnation:

> *Departed this life on Monday afternoon, Mr. Arthur Smith; and on Tuesday morning Mr. Thomas Hutson—young gentlemen were deposited in the tomb...A challenge had been given and accepted—a duel was fought...Such honor are thy triumphs! Come hither Duelist, and regale thy senses! See two young men...leveling the deadly tube at each other...See them groaning on a deathbed; and now they breathe their last. Hear the distracted outcries of a fond and doting parent...Oh thou idol, who delightest in human sacrifice; who snuffest up blood as sweet smelling incense; when will thy reign cease? Oh ye votaries of this Moloch, ye abetters of murder and bloodshed.*

An 1812 anti-dueling ordinance also failed to stop the killing. The act provided that any party to a duel would be subject to a two-thousand-dollar fine and imprisonment. Nobody much cared. In fact, one of the most popular dueling grounds in Charleston was at the Washington Racecourse, a short ride from City Hall.

For every man who reveled in these affairs of honor, there were many more who dreaded it. Violence was often averted thanks to successful mediation or the parties' willingness to give and accept "satisfaction" in the form of a proper retraction. If the apology was not accepted, there would be a challenge—and avoiding a challenge wasn't easy. Men who refused to fight would be "posted." An invitation to duel would be published in a newspaper or hung in a public place. One nineteenth-century observer asserted than any man that refused to accept the challenge would "never again be permitted to join gentleman even in a fox hunt. He's utterly out of it."

When Colonel McKinnon of Charleston refused to meet in a duel, he was shunned by his contemporaries and left town for good. William H. Drayton was challenged by General Charles Lee but declined. He basically ignored the challenge, stating he had no interest in ruining his own character or risking his life to indulge the stupidity of General Lee. Likewise, Robert Barnwell Rhett refused to duel on moral grounds. He later wrote of that decision, "I fear God more than I fear man. True courage is best evidenced by firm maintenance of our principals [*sic*] amidst all temptations." Such acts of courage were rare in Charleston where men fought without fear of the law or God.

Dueling protocol ruled most conflicts between individuals of a certain social standing. Nowhere is this more apparent than in the Brooks-Sumner affair. In May of 1856, Senator Charles Sumner of Massachusetts spent three days on the Senate floor criticizing president Franklin Pierce and the institution of slavery. His rhetorical attacks reached a climax with a speech in which Sumner coined the phrase "The Crime Against Kansas." This was his incendiary crescendo, a brilliant oration given over the course of two days, during which he declared that South Carolina suffered from a "shameful imbecility from Slavery." Before the packed Senate galleries, Sumner singled out Senator Andrew Butler for particular ridicule, referring to him as the Don Quixote with his Dulcinea, who "has chosen a mistress to whom he has made his vows, and who, though ugly to others, is always lovely to him...the harlot, Slavery." Sumner could not let it end there. He mocked Butler's speech impediment, declaring he "touches nothing which he does not disfigure with error, sometimes of principle, sometimes of fact. He cannot open his mouth, but out there flies a blunder."

Watching the speech from the gallery was Preston S. Brooks, a cousin of Butler who had been elected to the House from South Carolina. Seething, he at once resolved "to relieve Butler and avenge the insult to my State." But in Brooks's estimation, Sumner was not a gentleman and was unworthy of being challenged to a duel. He would have to find another way.

He proceeded to do just that. On the afternoon of May 22, 1856, Brooks found Sumner writing at his desk in a nearly empty Senate chamber. Clutching a cane with a gold head, Brooks walked up to Sumner and declared, "Mr. Sumner, I have read your speech twice over carefully. It is a libel on South Carolina, and Mr. Butler, who is a relative of mine." Just as Sumner started to stand, Brooks brought the cane down on his head with everything he had. Sumner was trapped at his desk and was defenseless to defend himself from the assault. Brooks continued battering the senator even after the bloodied Sumner broke free from

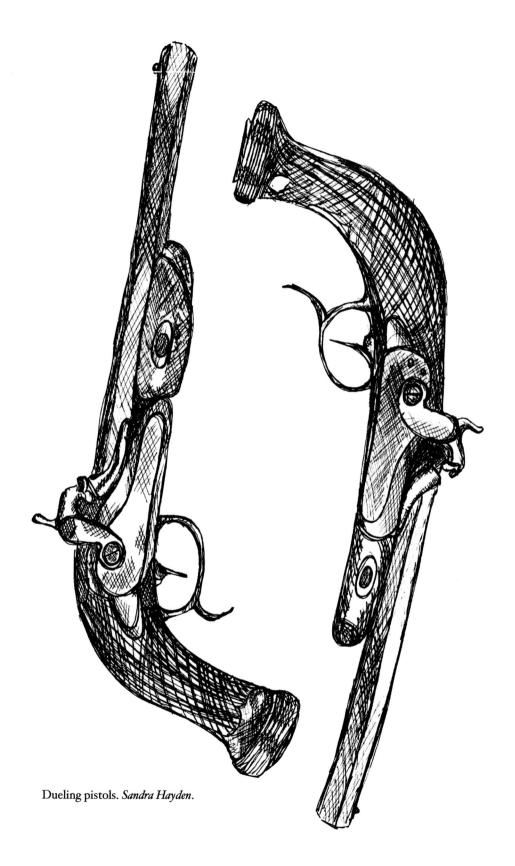

Dueling pistols. *Sandra Hayden*.

his desk and collapsed to the floor. Still unsatisfied, Brooks battered Sumner until the cane shattered in his hand.

Brooks became a sensation in South Carolina. As the House of Representatives voted (unsuccessfully) to eject Brooks from that body, he bragged, "Every Southern man sustains me. The fragments of the stick are begged for as sacred relicts." With his arrival in Charleston, he was presented with a new cane inscribed, "Hit him again," and Southern newspapers enthusiastically seconded the idea. Brooks had gotten his satisfaction.

Due to the combative nature of nineteenth-century politics, candidates and their critics were frequently drawn into affairs of honor. The more competitive a race, the more likely there was to be a duel. And no race was more competitive than the congressional election in the fall of 1856. After Edmund Rhett Jr. attacked candidate Judge A.G. Magrath anonymously in the *Charleston Mercury*, Judge Magrath's brother, Edward, exploded in anger. To restore his brother's reputation, Edward needed to make a dramatic public stand in defense of his honor. And nothing could be as dramatic as challenging both editors of the *Mercury*, who had printed the attack, to a duel.

According to the code of honor, Magrath could not challenge the editors without proof that they had impugned his brother's honor. As evidence, he cited the anonymous editorial in the *Mercury*, which attacked Judge Magrath's "bankrupt character." This editorial gave Edward Magrath all the evidence he needed to offer a challenge. He fired off a letter to editors John Heart and William R. Taber Jr., demanding satisfaction.

You have after repeated threatening & with deliberation, published and circulated insulting and libelous attacks upon my Brother Judge Magrath. To effect this; you have put aside the habitual decency of a Charleston newspaper & disregarding the taste & sentiments of the community have emulated the corruption & licentious of a venal press elsewhere...You have, it is true, attempted to interpose the protection of veil of an anonymous correspondent...for your supposed security may have sharpened the malice & stimulated the audacity of the attack...the intent of this communication is to afford you the opportunity of proving whether you did or did not calculate upon such immunity, and to demand the satisfaction recognized in such cases.

I invite you generally to a meeting & refer you for the necessary
arrangements to my friend...who will hand you this.
I am your obedient servant E Magrath

When editor William R. Taber Jr. received Edward Magrath's letter there was little doubt that a fight was coming. Magrath had essentially stated that the editors were responsible for anything that appeared in the pages of the *Charleston Mercury*. Taber was in a difficult spot. He didn't want to duel but he could not bring himself to apologize to Magrath. He also had to defend something larger than his life: freedom of the press. But most of all, it appears that he was deeply offended by Magrath's belligerent tone and wasn't about to back down. He abandoned any pretense of civility and sent a letter that he knew would bring things to a head.

You assume to represent the honor and manhood of your brother,
an avowed candidate for the highest office in our gift, and by
your interference reduce his honor and manhood to a vicarious
existence. I do not admit that when a candidate by his own
consent he can avoid the proper, necessary responsibilities of his
position as a candidate. If a judge, he is no less a candidate. He
cannot legitimately put his character in commission and maintain
his honor by proxy. If he can resign his seat to go to congress, he
can resign it, if necessary, to vindicate his honor. He has no right
to be a candidate if he ceases to be a man. But truth shall not be
muzzled, though he be a judge, and the liberty of the press shall be
maintained, even against the vicarious champion of his manhood
and the intrusive representative of his honor. This much for your
warrant to represent your brother and insult me.

Taber's letter was essentially a taunt to Magrath. First, Judge Magrath, not his brother, was obliged to seek satisfaction. To have a surrogate fight in your stead was cowardly. Second, Taber was obliged as a journalist to provide the truth and if the truth was insulting to Magrath, then so be it. There was no equivocation. And then he ends with a blustering statement that if things don't work out, he's ready for whatever may come. At this point, there was no turning back. A flurry of letters were sent back and forth and Rhett, the avowed author of the insulting editorial, stepped forward to accept responsibility. But Edward

Magrath was only interested in killing Taber at this point. Matters were further inflamed when Taber's second, Cunningham, wrote a final letter and essentially lectured Magrath, stating that they were ready to "seek satisfaction as well as give it."

Angry and insulted, Magrath demanded to know when and where the duel should take place. There seems to have been some difficulty nailing down the specifics and determining who had good dueling pistols, but there was no doubt where they were headed. After difficult negotiations, the specifics of how the duel was to be executed were agreed to and signed by both men:

> *Arrangements for a meeting between Mr. Taber and Mr. E Magrath.*
> *The distance to be ten paces or thirty feet — the weapons pistols —*
> *the place the Race Course — the time half past four PM Monday*
> *afternoon the 29th — the Pistols to be held muzzle down.*

The entire town was abuzz with news of the impending duel. Even Judge Magrath tried to stop it, but he arrived too late. According to one of his friends, nobody tried to intervene.

> *The time, place and circumstances of the proposed duel were known*
> *throughout the city. Magistrates knew them, the conservators of*
> *the peace knew them, pious men and even clergymen were as well*
> *acquainted with the facts as the parties interested.*

On the afternoon of September 29, 1856, William Taber and Edward Magrath, accompanied by their seconds, arrived at the Washington Racecourse. Once Taber and Magrath had loaded their pistols, the rules mandated that they take up their positions thirty feet apart. When the signal was given, they had three seconds to fire. Both men fired and missed. While the pistols were being reloaded, the seconds moved to end the duel but to no avail. Again the men fired and missed one another. As the *Code Duello* prescribed, a second and more rigorous effort was undertaken to settle the matter. Magrath was not going to be satisfied with a simple apology from William Taber. He wanted Taber to retract every word written about Judge Magrath. Taber flatly refused to concede to this demand, saying it was a matter of journalistic principle. With negotiations at an impasse, the men once again faced off, pistols in hand. On the third round of shots, Taber was killed.

Now John Heart, associate editor of the *Charleston Mercury*, stepped forward to duel Magrath. "I am ready to answer your demand for satisfaction," Heart said as he watched Taber's body being dragged from the field. Rhett was also present and ready to take his place if Heart fell.

After a quick conference with his second, Magrath answered that he had no further demands to make and left the field. Ironically, shooting Taber, which Magrath thought would restore his brother's reputation, instead tarnished it. In the wake of the killing, Judge Magrath withdrew from the congressional race and retired from public life until the matter had blown over. But in the meantime, Taber's friends screamed for revenge. In an effort to goad Magrath's second into an affair of honor, Thomas Stuart wrote a letter blaming him for delivering the belligerent correspondence that provoked the duel.

> [T]*hat letter was a most informal letter for one gentleman to hand another...More than that, I now write to inform you, that whether from desire of being known as a torpedo; whether from your own malice, or calculations, whether you have been a foolish tool of calculating set, or, what not, you nevertheless, as the communicating medium of that letter, stand forth in bold relief, as the prime agent of Taber's enemies, to the directing of that letter which has destroyed his life. Sir, you are guilty of blood, which you yourself, had not the courage to take; you have tampered with life by the gross violation of the laws of chivalry; you have murdered my friend.*

Eventually things began to settle down and the view of most Charlestonians was probably captured by the editor of the *Central Presbyterian* when he wrote:

> *A duel settles no principals* [sic], *elects no truth, vindicates no innocence, proves no man brave. Why should "The Code" be called a "Code of Honor," which violates the laws of God and Man?*

By the time Taber was killed in the fall of 1856, the public had grown weary of dueling. With his murder, the people at last were disgusted with it, and they showed their contempt. And it would soon disappear altogether from Charleston. But it was too late for William Taber.

A FATAL GOLDEN SEED

The precise year Jonack Lynch emigrated from Ireland to America is uncertain, but it likely coincided with the early settlement of Charles Towne. Similarly, we can only speculate on his reasons for moving to the New World: a strong desire to emulate the character, condition, style and wealth of his aristocratic ancestors. Lynch, like many of Charles Towne's earliest inhabitants, carved his first plantation, Blessing, from the virgin forest and built himself a modest home overlooking the Cooper River. He was a wayfarer in the wilderness, and neither his previous environment nor his social status would have accustomed him to the depredations and dangers of the frontier. It was a hard life, as any frontier life must be, but not without its rewards. Blessing's profits allowed Lynch and his descendants to acquire additional lands in the young colony and rise to a high position among Charles Towne's planter elite.

Upon his death, Jonack Lynch left his son Thomas (born ca. 1675) a slight inheritance, which, "through industry and the purchase of a large tract of land devoted to the cultivation of rice, was increased to an impressive fortune." By the first decade of the eighteenth century, his holdings had grown to include seven plantations and more than two hundred slaves. Thomas Lynch's most productive plantations were on

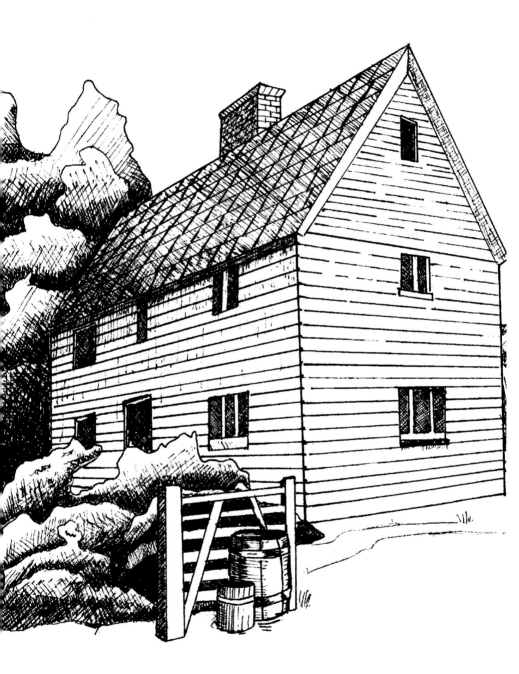

Lynch plantation house. *Nick Hendrix.*

the Santee River, that fertile stream that would provide the basis of the family fortunes.

Despite the family's seasonal migration to the Charles Towne peninsula, their permanent residence remained the Lynch plantation in Christ Church Parish. Thomas Lynch built himself a proper home on a low bluff above the upper confluence of the Wando River and Horlbeck Creek.

It must have been a satisfying time for Thomas Lynch. The young planter could look north to south with pride, the prospect of prosperity expanding around him—the result of great enterprise, and much of it the product of his own fertile imagination.

But the plantation was not cleared and cultivated by imagination alone. Lynch had eagerly moved to acquire slaves to complete this formidable task. During his first two decades in Carolina, Native Americans worked on Lynch's plantation alongside a few African slaves brought from Barbados and even, occasionally, white indentured servants. After rice planting took hold in the 1690s, Lynch brought in a large African workforce familiar with rice production and resistant to tropical diseases. The majority of those slaves were taken from a part of Africa that extended along the West African coastline from Senegal to Angola and perhaps as far as five hundred miles into the interior.

From his first years scratching it out on the frontier, Lynch would emerge as one of the wealthiest men in South Carolina. Rice would build his mansions, educate his children and form the basis of his wealth. But to sustain his prosperity, Lynch would have to rely on a foreign and disaffected workforce. And to grow his fortune, Lynch would resort to brutality to extract the requisite labor from his African slaves. As he increased the pressure, his slaves began to run from his plantation with increased frequency. Advertisements in Charleston's newspapers often mentioned runaways "well marked by whipping."

Not infrequently, slaves of both sexes, pushed to the limit, attacked and killed white people, including their overseers and masters. Newspaper and court records give innumerable accounts of poisonings, arson and physical assaults committed by slaves as they pushed back against their domination. The *Georgia Gazette* reported on "a most shocking murder committed a few weeks ago...by a Negro fellow belonging to one John Meyer who happened to come to Charleston." According to the paper, "the cruel wretch murdered Mrs. Meyer, her daughter about 16 years of age, and her suckling infant; he then dressed himself in his master's best clothes, and set fire to the house, which was burnt to the ground." Three of the Meyer children slipped away before being discovered and alerted the neighbors. The unnamed slave was apprehended the next day and was "condemned to be burnt alive at the stake, which was accordingly executed."

Reprisals against slaves were swift and brutal. The authorities made a public spectacle of "saucy slaves," who they tortured, castrated, whipped and publicly executed. In July 1769, a slave name Dolly and another called "the Doctor" were convicted of poisoning James Sands and his wife and child. With a mob gathered to watch the gruesome event, they were burned at the stake in downtown Charles Town. Another slave was accused of instigating the crime and was "adjudged to receive twenty-five Lashes on Saturday Morning at four different Corners and the same last Tuesday, in all 100 each Day, and to lose his Right Ear."

Sometimes plantation owners decided to forgo the legal system and administer "justice" at their own discretion. When clergyman St. John De Crevecoeur visited South Carolina during the colonial period, he recorded one of the most graphic and horrifying accounts of slave punishment on record:

I was not long since invited to dine with a planter who lived three miles from Charles Towne, where he then resided. In order to avoid the heat of the sun, I resolved to go on foot, sheltered in some small path, leading through a pleasant wood. I was leisurely travelling along, attentively examining some peculiar plants which I had collected, when all at once I felt the air strongly agitated, though the day was perfectly calm and sultry. I immediately cast my eyes toward the cleared ground, from which I was but a small distance, in order to see whether it was not occasioned by a sudden shower; when at that instant a sound resembling a deep rough voice, uttered, as I thought, a few inarticulate monosyllables. Alarmed and surprised, I precipitately looked all round, when I perceived at about six rods distance something resembling a cage, suspended to the limbs of a tree; all of the branches of which appeared covered with large birds of prey, fluttering about, and anxiously endeavoring to perch on the cage. Actuated by an involuntary motion of my hands, more than by any design of my mind, I fired at them; they all flew a short distance, with a most hideous noise: when, horrid to think and painful to repeat, I perceived a negroe, suspended in the cage and left there to expire! I shudder when I recollect that the birds had already picked out his eyes, his cheek bones were bare; his arms had been attacked in several places, and his body seemed covered with a multitude of wounds. From the edges of the hollow sockets and from the laceration with which he was disfigured, the blood slowly dropped, and tinged the ground beneath. No sooner were the birds flown, than swarms of insects covered the whole body of this unfortunate wretch, eager to feed on his mangled flesh and to drink his blood. I found myself suddenly arrested by the power of affright and terror; my nerves were convulsed; I trembled, I stood motionless, involuntarily contemplating the fate of this Negro, in all its dismal latitude. The living spectre, though deprived of his eyes, could still distinctly hear, and in his uncouth dialect begged me to give him some water to allay his thirst. Humanity herself would have recoiled back with horror; she would have balanced whether to lessen such relief less distress, or mercifully with one blow to end this dreadful scene of agonizing torture! Had I a ball in my gun, I certainly should have dispatched him; but finding myself unable to perform so kind an office, I sought though trembling to relieve him as well as I could. A shell ready fixed to a pole, which had been used by some Negroes, presented itself to me; filled it with water, and with trembling hands I guided it to the quivering lips of the wretched sufferer. Urged by the irresistible power of thirst, he endeavored to meet it, as he instinctively guessed its approach by the noise it made passing through the bars of the cage. "Tanke, you white man, tanke you, pute some poison and give me." "How long have you been hanging there?" I asked him. "Two days, and me no die; the birds, aaah me!" Oppressed with the reflections which this shocking spectacle afforded me, I mustered strength enough to walk away, and soon reached the house at which I intended to dine. There I heard that the reason for this slave being thus punished, was on account of his having killed the overseer of the plantation. They told me that the laws of self-preservation rendered such executions necessary; and supported the doctrine of slavery with the arguments generally made use of to justify the practice; with the repetition of which I shall not trouble you at present. (Adier)

De Crevecoeur was not the only clergyman to take notice of the inherent cruelties common to slavery in South Carolina. When Reverend Charles Wesley visited Charleston in August of 1736, he recounted several stories of the cruelties committed against slaves. Among those credited with the worst offenses was none other than Thomas Lynch.

Mon., August 2d.

I had observed much, and heard more, of the cruelty of masters towards their negroes; but now I received an authentic account of some horrid instances thereof. The giving a child a slave of its own age to tyrannize over, to beat and abuse out of sport, was, I myself saw, a common practice. Nor is it strange, being thus trained up in cruelty, they should afterwards arrive at so great perfection in it; that Mr. Star, a gentleman I often met at Mr. Lasserre's, should, as he himself informed L., first nail up a negro by the ears, then order him to be whipped in the severest manner, and then to have scalding water thrown over him, so that the poor creature could not stir for four months after. Another much-applauded punishment is, drawing their slaves' teeth. One Colonel Lynch is universally known to have cut off a poor negro's legs; and to kill several of them every year by his barbarities.

It were endless to recount all the shocking instances of diabolical cruelty which these men (as they call themselves) daily practise upon their fellow-creatures; and that on the most trivial occasions. I shall only mention one more, related to me by a Swiss gentleman, Mr. Zouberbuhler, an eye-witness, of Mr. Hill, a dancing-master in Charlestown. He whipped a she-slave so long, that she fell down at his feet for dead. When, by the help of a physician, she was so far recovered as to show signs of life, he repeated the whipping with equal rigour, and concluded with dropping hot sealing-wax upon her flesh. Her crime was overfilling a tea-cup.

These horrid cruelties are the less to be wondered at, because the government itself, in effect, countenances and allows them to kill their slaves, by the ridiculous penalty appointed for it, of about seven pounds sterling, half of which is usually saved by the criminal's informing against himself. This I can look upon as no other than a public act to indemnify murder.

By the 1730s, the situation had grown dangerously out of control. But that was the central contradiction of Charles Town. To enjoy the prosperity of the soil, planters like Thomas Lynch had to discipline a growing and angry workforce to the harsh injustices of slavery. They also had to live in constant terror at the prospect of being murdered by their own laborers. By the 1730s, the large number of African slaves living in Charles Town had grown so great that a missionary working at Christ Church Parish ominously stated that "the people are forced to come to church with Guns loaded." The stage was now set for the biggest slave uprising in North American history.

Under the leadership of a slave named Jemmy, a group of twenty Angolan slaves began their journey to St. Augustine on the evening of Sunday, September 9, 1739. Seeking to first gather weapons and supplies, they launched several attacks on local storehouses and dwellings clustered around the Stono River. Their first target was Hutchenson's storehouse at Stono Bridge. Without warning, the slaves burst into the building and murdered and decapitated storekeepers Robert Bathurst and Mr. Gibbs, leaving their heads on the stairs. That grisly work done, the Africans ransacked the building and made off with a large quantity of gunpowder and weapons. Now armed, they set out along Rantowle's Road and "plundered and burnt Mr. Godfrey's house, and killed him, his Daughter and Son."

As the sun was rising over the marshes of Rantowles Creek, they arrived at a cluster of houses surrounding Wallace's tavern. The white inhabitants saw them coming, but nobody tried to stop them; nobody could. Though the innkeeper at the tavern was spared, for "he was a good man and kind to his Slaves," the Africans plundered the house of Mr. Lemy and killed him, his wife and child. The house was then burnt to the ground. The rebels then spread out over the neighborhood and "marched towards Mr. Roses resolving to kill him; but he was saved by a Negroe, who having hid him went out and pacified the others." The armed slaves were growing more confident and decided to forgo any pretense of stealth. As they marched south, the rebels called out, "Liberty," and marched on with Colours displayed, and two drums beating." They burned houses, killed livestock, scattered possessions and decapitated the dead and dying before moving to the next plantation. Now seemingly indestructible, their numbers swelled and perhaps as many as fifty marched along Rantowle's Road, "pursuing all the white people they met with, and killing Man, Woman, and Child when they could come to them." It was a full-fledged rebellion.

The rebels caught the Lowcountry's white population by surprise. Many would have been on their way to church, allowing their slaves to pursue their own activities on that morning. Thomas Elliott, a prosperous planter from the Rantowles Creek neighborhood, was just returning from the Baptist church when he stumbled on the rebels. According to a petition submitted after the rebellion, Elliott and his family would have surely perished that day if not for the actions of a single slave named July.

> *That upon Inquiry your Committee find that a Negro man named July belonging to Mr Thomas Elliott was very early and chiefly instrumental in saving his Master and his Family from being destroyed by the Rebellious Negroes and that the Negro man July had at several times bravely fought against the Rebels and killed one of them. Your Committee therefore recommends that the* [said] *Negro July (as a reward for his faithful Services and for Encouragement to other Slaves to follow his Example in case of the like Nature) shall have his Freedom and a Present of a Suit of Cloaths, Shirt, Hat, a pair of stockings and a pair of Shoes.*

Returning to Charles Town for the legislative session from his plantation in Prince William Parish, Lieutenant Governor William Bull also stumbled across the slaves traveling northward along the Pons Pons Road. Turning his horse just before coming into range of the muskets, Bull rode at full speed to alert the militia. The slaves fired a few shots then proceeded to Alexander Hext's plantation at Caw Caw Swamp, where they killed the overseer and his wife before burning the buildings to the ground. Hext's neighbors fared no better; the rebels "burnt Mr. Sprye's house, and then Mr. Sacheverall's and then Mr. Nash's house, all lying on the Pons Pons Road and killed all the white people they found in them."

As dusk approached on Sunday evening, the slaves had marched ten miles and had "burnt all before them without any opposition." With every mile traveled, their numbers "increased every minute by New Negroes coming to them," until nearly a hundred had joined their ranks. By the time they approached the Edisto River, much of the contingent had consumed excessive quantities of the "Rum they had taken in the Houses" or were intoxicated by the excitement and violence that had occurred throughout the day. Thinking they were now victorious over the whole province, they collected in a field near the Jacksonborough Ferry, rejoicing in their freedom by "dancing, Singing, and Beating Drums." As night approached, the slaves began to relax, unaware of any need for caution. They had defeated their masters.

News of the attacks quickly reached Charles Town and the militia was summoned. Although outnumbered by their slaves, the white inhabitants of Charles Town were well armed, and most had fought in wars against the Native Americans where they learned to count on swiftness, mobility and terror, with the assurance that discipline and firepower could overcome superior numbers. The militia, numbering over "One hundred Planters," set up guards on the crossroads and began patrolling the vicinity to prevent the slaves from slipping into the swamps and thickets. With all exits covered, they isolated the rebels on Wadmalaw Island and set out to crush the rising in one decisive battle.

The militia located the rebels east of the Edisto River, where they had just set fire to the main house at Battlefield Plantation. With the whites speedily advancing on their position, "their black captain, named Cato, who had two loaded guns immediately discharged one," and was reaching down to grab another musket when he was gunned down. Trapped in an open field, the slaves were vulnerable. A few of the rebels probably had some experience in intertribal fighting in Africa, but they were not prepared or sufficiently armed to stand against well-aimed musket fire. The militia spread out along a wide front and poured a shower of lead into the gathering of slaves. According to one account, fourteen slaves fell on that first salvo. Standing against a veritable firestorm, the slaves scattered and retreated to the safety of the woods. Many of the Africans rallied in the forest and decided to win or die on the spot, though dying was the far more likely outcome. Although one witness reported that the slaves "behaved boldly," the rebels were ridden down by militia horsemen who shot and hacked at will once panic set in.

"The militia," claimed one observer, "did not torture one Negro, but only put them to an easy Death." According to one contemporary, "About fifty of these villains attempted to go home but were taken by the Planters who cut off their heads and set them up at every Mile Post they came to." The last fatality was in December 1742, when "one of the Ringleaders of the last Negro Insurrection, was lately seized in Cawcaw Swamp, by two Negro Fellows that ran away from Mr. Grimke, who brought him to Stono, where he was immediately hang'd."

The rebellion left an estimated twenty-five whites and over seventy slaves dead and more than fifteen plantations sacked and razed. But the mayhem of the day set in motion events that transformed the colony into an even more brutal and cruel place than before. The authorities responded to the rebellion by enacting a series of draconian laws meant

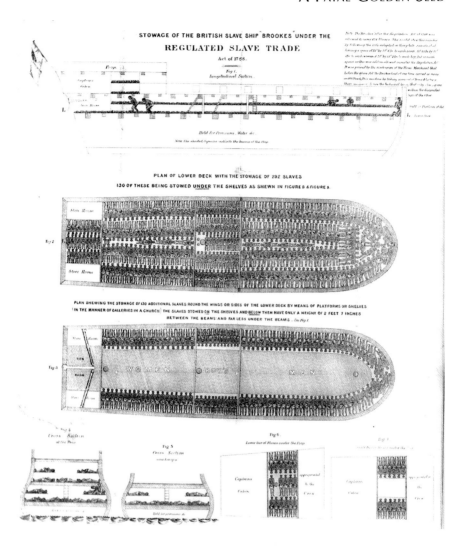

Plan of a British slave ship. *Library of Congress.*

to destroy the very spirit of their slaves. Any hint of restlessness was cause for the most gruesome punishments. The Carolinians briefly halted the slave trade but there was no real effort to reform the foundation of their wealth. In the words of one Carolinian on the eve of the American Civil War, "Slavery is our King—Slavery is our Truth—Slavery is our Divine Right."

It would take another 125 years and the lives of 618,000 Americans in the Civil War to finally rid the country of the "Peculiar Institution."

BORN FIGHTING:
THE BORDER REIVERS
OF FENWICK HALL

O come with me, Ghosts walk tonight,
Victims of bloody border fight
Who made our English history,
Grey phantom Percies lead the way
Against the Douglas chivalry,
Grey ghosts of ancient mystery.
Lo! Watch them sweep o'er Flodden Field,
Where all the flowers of Scotland died;
Death cannot slay the splendid pride
Of those who fell but scorned to yield,
Who fought in vain, except to earn
Their name upon the scroll of fame
And write in blood each hero's name
Upon the stones of Otterburn.

Frederick C. Palmer
The Ghosts

U ntil England and Scotland were united under a single king in March
1603, the border between them was a natural place for anarchy,

devastation and slaughter. The two countries had been warring for centuries, and the border land was ravaged again and again by invading armies and quarreling neighbors. The clans living along that miserable stretch received no protection from their governments. They turned to lawlessness to survive, taking what they needed with disregard for rules and valuing family over country. Cattle rustling, blackmail, extortion, murder, arson and pillaging were all common occurrences along the border. As George MacDonald Fraser explains in his book *The Steel Bonnets*:

> *While the monarchs of England and Scotland ruled the comparatively secure hearts of their kingdoms, the narrow hill land between was dominated by the lance and the sword. The tribal leaders from their towers, the broken men, and outlaws of the mosses, the ordinary peasants of the valleys, in their own phrase, "shook loose the Border". They continued to shake it as long as it was political reality, practising systematic robbery and destruction on each other. History has christened them the Border Reivers.*

The life of the border reiver was not ruled by his allegiance to the English or Scottish crown, but by his allegiance to the family. The border reivers were often either farmers or landholders, but reiving was not limited to any particular social class. Many nobles were themselves some of the most notorious raiders. Among the gentry that lived off plunder and murder were the Fenwicks.

Appearing on the Scottish border around 1220, Robert de Ffenwick is the first recorded owner of the surname. The next recorded Fenwicks are Walter del Feneweke in Lincolnshire, 1275, and Thomas de Fenwyck of Northumberland in 1279. They are thought to take their name from Kyloe in Northumberland, a name that means "the farm on the fen."

The Fenwicks lived on both sides of the border. Numbering "five hundred in a flock," the Northumberland and Scottish Fenwicks were famous for their ruthlessness. There are numerous accounts of betrayal and perjury, and their raids are too numerous to list. Their original seat was at Fenwick Tower, but from the time of Henry IV, their principal castle was at Wallington. Here the Fenwicks raided and thieved from their neighbors in a constant cycle of feud and revenge.

Like the Celtic warrior, the Fenwicks glorified their raids in elaborate and often highly poetic ballads. British historian George

M. Trevelyan summed up the nature of the border reivers and their ballads when he wrote:

> *They were cruel, coarse savages, slaying each other like the beasts of the forest; and yet they were also poets who could express in the grand style the inexorable fate of the individual man and woman, the infinite pity for all cruel things which they none the less inflicted upon one another. It was not one ballad-maker alone but the whole cut throat population who felt this magnanimous sorrow, and the consoling charms of the highest poetry.*

But the borders were not always filled with tales of the Fenwicks' exploits in battle. The Fenwicks' castle at Northumberland was the setting of Sir Walter Scott's famous ballad *Young Lochinvar*, in which the Fenwicks and their feuding cousins, the Foresters, unsuccessfully pursued a daughter of the clan who had eloped with a Scottish rogue:

> *There was mounting 'mong Graemes of the Netherby Clan,*
> *Fosters, Fenwicks and Musgraves, they rode and they ran;*
> *There was racing and chasing on Cannonbie Lea,*
> *But the lost bride of Netherby ne'er did they see!*
> *So daring in love, and so dauntless in war,*
> *Have ye e'er heard of gallant like young Lochinvar?*

Having their failure immortalized in English literature must have been galling for the ancient Fenwick family.

After three hundred years as reivers, the Fenwicks became expert light horsemen, skilled in raiding, scouting, ambushing and skirmishing. Like many of the other border reivers, the Fenwicks were cursed in both countries as "evell disposed personnes, Inclined to wildness and disorder." Though despised in peacetime, the Fenwicks were eagerly recruited by the English in times of war. It was said that the "most remarkable of the mounted men in Henry VIll's [sic] army were the Northem Horsemen who, having been called into existence by the eternal forays of the Scottish Border were light cavalry, probably fhe very best in Europe."

By the sixteenth century, the Fenwick name had become synonymous with horses. From their estate in Northumberland, they raised the finest horses in all of Britain. They became so acclaimed in equestrian circles that Sir John Fenwick was made master of the horse to King Charles I.

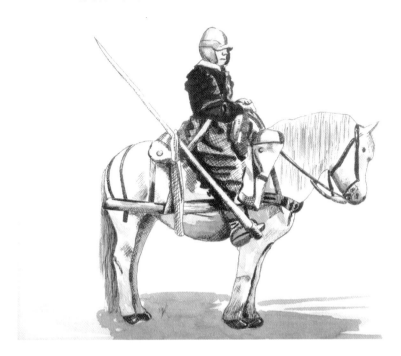

The border reiver. *Nick Hendrix.*

Inevitably, the Fenwicks were drawn into the ruthless politics of the day. According to one historian of the Fenwick clan:

> *During the Civil War, a Northumbrian called Sir John Fenwick was killed at Marston Moor, but it is a descendant of the same name, who lived during the reign of King William of Orange, who has gained greater fame. This Sir John Fenwick was beheaded for High Treason after conspiring to murder the Dutch born protestant King. Sir John's property and estate were confiscated by King William, who came into possession of Fenwick's horse called Sorrel. This horse was later to throw the King from its saddle after it stumbled near a mole hill in the grounds of Hampton Court. Shortly afterwards King William died from his injuries. The horse had thus fulfilled the wishes of its original master.*

The accession of James VI to the English throne brought an end to the reign of the reivers. After the reivers relieved his English subjects of some 1,280 cattle and 3,840 sheep and goats, James issued a proclamation against "all rebels and disorderly persons." Those not on the receiving end of "Jethart Justice," which amounted to hanging without trial, were deported or forced to fight for the king's armies.

The scattering of the border reivers coincided with the English settlement of the New World and many sons of the Fenwick clan were obliged to seek prosperity on the American frontier. But it is not likely that any could lay claim to adventures more strange and romantic than those which befell a branch that came to South Carolina.

Born in Northumberland, England, John Fenwick came to the fledgling province sometime in the 1690s. He may have dreamed of lush fields of crops, but during his first years in Carolina, John worked in Charles Towne as a rice merchant and Indian trader. His business ventures were a tremendous success, and he soon enjoyed a profitable trade with the West Indies and Britain. With an eye to expanding his estate, he married Elizabeth Gibbes, whose massive dowry and name helped complete Fenwick's transformation from an ambitious young bachelor to a Carolina gentleman. Between 1690 and 1715, John Fenwick acquired two thousand acres on Johns Island and seven hundred acres at the mouth of the Ashepoo River, including seven plantations and more than five hundred slaves.

By 1730, John Fenwick had built himself a proper mansion on Johns Island. From the Stono River, a visitor might have seen Fenwick Hall with its considerable open ground dotted with slave quarters and barns, constructed mostly of heavy timber, beautified with flourishing orchards and fields. Burgeoning virgin forest provided a wild and solemn backdrop to the plantation setting. One or two roads wound around the estate, turning off to visit every building, and at the termination of the open country was a Georgian mansion, strongly built of brick and timber. The house's southern orientation provided sunlight for warmth in the winter and maximum exposure to the prevailing winds during the warmer months. It was an astounding architectural achievement, even by the standards of Charles Town.

Despite the family's rapid rise to prosperity in Carolina, it was rumored that the Fenwicks continued their reiver ways. In fact, Robert Fenwick, brother of John, was a scoundrel of the worst sort. He had taken up the family tradition of thievery, working as a pirate and plundering "heathen vessels" in the Indian Ocean. There was not much concern in the New World over Fenwick's occupation until his ship appeared in the colonists' own backyard off the coast of Pennsylvania. Vigorously pursued from that northern coast, Fenwick sailed into Charles Towne in 1692 aboard the *Loyal Jamaica*, which had been taken from the French as a prize of war. It was a smart move. Piracy flourished in South Carolina under the protection of officials of the province. So well did the city's merchants and the "Red Sea Men," as the pirates were politely called, understand one another, that the buccaneers became a common sight in Charles Towne toward the end of the seventeenth century. For a brief period, Charles Towne became a known port of refuge where pirate booty could be disposed of at enormous gains with no questions asked.

Gossip abounded in the Johns Island community that Fenwick Hall had become Robert Fenwick's secret hiding place. It was quietly whispered that he had graduated to robbing the Atlantic fleets and that he cared not whether the vessel flew a Spanish or British flag. The entire family was said to be enjoying the proceeds of his theft. Though it certainly had no factual basis, legend held that a tunnel had been constructed from the Stono River to Fenwick Hall so that the family might secret the stolen goods without the neighbors seeing, or make a safe escape if the authorities ever came knocking.

Charles Town's tolerance of pirates was all to end very suddenly. The colonists grew tired of the pirates and decided to kill or capture them whenever they neared. With the Charles Town authorities scouring the southern waters in a determined effort to put down buccaneering, pirating was becoming bad business. Briefly imprisoned after running the *Loyal Jamaica* aground in Sewee Bay, Robert Fenwick thought it wise to give up life on the sea. In Charles Town, he soon built himself a fine home, married and joined the Presbyterian Church. He became a force in both politics and in Charles Town society, serving as commissioner of the Indian trade, captain in the militia and justice of the peace. Nevertheless, Robert's exploits were a period in family history that no one wished to remember.

By the second decade of the eighteenth century, the family had become the unchallenged masters of Johns Island. The descendant of a family steeped in the tradition of horse racing, and in a sound financial situation, John Fenwick decided to build a large racecourse on the island. It was laid out in a wide track, extending from the mansion along the public road to St. Johns Church. Fenwick returned to England to purchase several horses of "Fenwick's Arabian Race" from his relatives. The Thoroughbred is a breed of horse that descends from three foundation sires: the Byerly Turk, the Godolphin Arabian and the Darley Arabian. The stallions, named for their owners, were taken to England from the Middle East around 1600 and bred to native Scottish Galloways. Matchem, foaled in England and grandson of the Godolphin

Arabian, was brought to Johns Island by Fenwick where he dominated South Carolina racing for a decade.

Quiet and stern by nature, John Fenwick ruled Fenwick Hall by his own decrees. He had a reputation for being just, but ruthless when necessary. Those in his employ were cowed by his powerful personality, but he was always kind and indulgent with his children, whom he spoiled. Especially close to Fenwick's heart was his daughter, Ann. She shared his love of horses, and they would often ride together, talking the way fathers and daughters do.

One day, seventeen-year-old Ann approached her father with the news that she had fallen in love. The object of her affections was a stable hand that had been hired to work with the family's impressive Arabian horses. Tony and Ann often spent time riding together after John left the stables in the morning to attend to plantation business. Tony had come to Carolina with adventure in his heart, a handsome young man who himself was an impressive horseman—exactly the kind of person to awaken Ann's impulsive affection. When at last John Fenwick grew angry and asked what they found to talk about on those long rides, Ann told him that they planned to marry. In the euphoria of the moment, it was natural for Ann to think of herself and Tony united happily in the future with the blessing of her father. Perhaps she thought her father would welcome such a splendid plan; more likely she thought he would simply accept it. But John Fenwick would hear none of it. The daughter of a Fenwick married to a stable hand was an absurdity. He severely flogged the boy and sent him off from the plantation.

John Fenwick may have thought that the thing was as good as settled, but that it is not how the heart works. Tony and Ann found a priest who married them, then they set off for Charles Town. Only a mile from town, the couple was unable to cross the Ashley River and found an abandoned cabin to spend their first night as man and wife. They waited that cool autumn night in constant fear, expecting John Fenwick's wrath—and John Fenwick's wrath, with good reason, was dreaded by everyone who knew him.

Up to this point, Fenwick had been indulgent to his daughter, but he was above all severe to those who opposed his will. It might not have mattered so much if it had been a purely personal disappointment, but it was far from that. A man of Fenwick's status could not accept the news of the marriage without losing honor, without being made to look foolish. Everyone on the plantation knew what had happened and they were waiting to see what he would do. Was it too late? Could the marriage be stopped? At that moment, Fenwick was trapped by his own pride and reputation, forced to do something that would severely injure his family—something that made him ashamed in his later life whenever he stopped to think about it.

John Fenwick set out at daybreak and tracked the couple to their Ashley River hideout. Johns Island legend has it that Tony was quickly seized and placed in a carriage with Ann. When they reached Fenwick Hall, Ann informed her father that they were already married and that there was nothing that could be done. She was wrong. Fenwick ordered the group to a nearby tree with a rope thrown over a branch. He had Tony mounted on a horse, and a noose slipped around his neck. Fenwick then placed a whip in his daughter's hands and compelled her to strike the horse. Ann pled desperately for Tony's life, but to no avail. She watched in horror as her groom slowly strangled to death. No magistrate was called, and there was no public outrage over the death of Tony. In the cruel and unforgiving world of colonial South Carolina, a murder in the name of honor went virtually unnoticed. As in Northumberland, the Fenwicks were a law unto themselves.

In 1746, John Fenwick returned to his ancestral home in Cumberland County, England, leaving his massive estate "whole and intire" to his son Edward. Edward Fenwick, known as Lord Ripon, sailed for Carolina and brought ten of the finest Arabian horses of the Fenwick stock. Once he arrived, he elaborated on his father's stables and established the Johns Island Stud, boasting the best horses in America. Even by the high standards of the Fenwick clan, Lord Ripon stood alone in his love of horses, and became the founder of The Turf in Carolina and co-founder of the original South Carolina Jockey Club.

Just as the American Revolution was beginning in earnest, Lord Ripon moved to New York to seek a better climate for a chronic respiratory illness. While he lay on his deathbed, his oldest son Edward asked permission to marry the daughter of Colonel John Stuart, the British superintendent of Indian affairs and "a determined enemy of the revolutionary party." In his official capacity, Stuart was said to have negotiated with the Cherokee to attack the South Carolina colonists. Though his father vehemently objected to the union, Edward followed through with the marriage to Stuart's daughter. When Lord Ripon was informed of the marriage, he struck Edward from his will and placed his estate in the hands of Robert Gibbes, a relative and devout Patriot. Denied his considerable inheritance,

Edward Fenwick grew everyday more resentful and soon conspired with his younger brother to join the British ranks.

The treason of Thomas and Edward Fenwick had been long premeditated. Constantly persuaded that they were neglected and ill treated by the Provincial Congress, who had jailed the brothers for aiding in the escape of Edward's mother-in-law at the outbreak of the American Revolution, their resentment grew extreme. To compound their anger, a petition was filed in the court of Chancery that their father's estate be divided among his other heirs for the misconduct of Edward and Thomas. By the time the petition was filed, their treacherous sentiments were fully grown, and they began a secret correspondence with the British.

Thomas and Edward Fenwick, who wished to injure the American cause while enhancing the value of their services to the British, applied for officer's commissions in the Johns Island militia, a post of the utmost value since this was the route the British had chosen to attack Charles Town. Being fine horsemen with an intimate knowledge of the Sea Islands, their application for this post was quickly granted. The brothers at once privately engaged to deliver Charles Town's southern flank to the enemy in exchange for an assurance that they would receive their inheritance and captain's commissions in the British Army.

The British first attempted to take Charles Town by sea, but were turned back in a ferocious battle at Fort Moultrie. They returned in the winter of 1780 when a major expeditionary force of ten thousand British and Hessian troops landed on Seabrook Island. The American forces were withdrawn to the city, and the British cavalry moved onto Johns Island, taking the plantations with virtually no resistance. To everyone's astonishment, the British were warmly received by the Fenwick bothers who offered their home as a base of operations.

By the time the English reached Fenwick Hall, the brothers had grown obsessed beyond all reason by their resentment and their feelings of persecution. They cared not in the least who ruled South Carolina, whether it was well or badly governed, prosperous or ravaged by war, free or under the dominion of the British Army—they wanted their birthright. As in Northumberland, the Fenwicks kept to a code of honor when it was in their best interests to do so.

Now at the head of a large contingent of British horsemen, Thomas Fenwick led an attack on a group of his own soldiers camped at Matthews Plantation. The Patriot militia was totally unprepared and more than eighty were attacked and routed. The surviving American forces, stuck in a hopeless situation, submitted to the British, surrendering and handing over their weapons. The British promised that if the militia members pledged not to take up arms against the crown anymore, they could return to their homes and remain unpunished. Once their arms were laid down, the British encircled the Americans and bayoneted the unarmed men. Their adrenaline high from the orgy of killing, the British then began to loot and burn all the homes and property that they came across.

That bloody work done, Thomas led a body of British cavalry to Peaceful Retreat, the home of the Gibbes family. The British took immediate possession of the house, leaving the premises to their men, and extending no protection against pillage. The soldiers stole at their pleasure, emptying the wine cellars, "drinking to intoxication, and seizing upon and carrying off the negroes." Among those forced out of the house were seven orphan children of Mrs. Fenwick, the presumed heirs of Fenwick Hall. After that treacherous day, the Fenwick brothers could not travel alone on Johns Island. Their neighbors wanted them dead.

During the last three years of the American Revolution numerous battles and skirmishes occurred throughout South Carolina as the British attempted to subdue the rebellion in the Southern theatre. The violence was all-consuming, pitting family against family and neighbor against neighbor, and murder and cruelty were the accepted methods for resolving matters. Thomas Fenwick led a group of troops that murdered suspected Patriots, ambushed American troops and plundered the homes of republican sympathizers. He became one of the most hated of all Loyalists in South Carolina.

On April 12, 1780, Thomas traveled south toward Fort Balfour with a contingent of thirty-five mounted dragoons. It was a dangerous trek for a man in Fenwick's situation. The South Carolina militia had ambushed and killed several British soldiers, and he did not care to fall into their hands. The King's Highway was the quickest route to the fort, but Thomas instead took a very circuitous route, cautiously prowling the back roads like an animal suspecting a trap. He sent out so many detachments and left so many garrisons at important points along the way to Balfour, that only seven men accompanied him on his journey.

With night quickly approaching, Thomas decided to rest for the night at the Vanbibers' house. It was a weary and restless night for Fenwick. He knew the South Carolina militia was lurking in the area and that he had so far done well to avoid them. Now he was stopping for the night without an adequate number of men to defend his position. At the first light of dawn he roused himself from his troubled sleep, woke the other soldiers and ordered the horses to be prepared for an early departure.

That same morning, ten men had stationed themselves in ambush on the road between the Vanbibers' and Fort Balfour with the object of intercepting suspicious persons, or discovering the movement of British troops. Three of them were concealed in the bushes near the Vanbiber house.

Just as Thomas Fenwick was finishing breakfast, the militia surrounded the house and sent word that he could surrender or they would burn the house with him inside. Fenwick gave up without firing a shot. He was then marched to Fort Balfour where Captain Harden of the South Carolina militia ordered the remaining British soldiers to lay down their weapons or be annihilated. Within two hours, eight British officers and sixty soldiers had surrendered themselves and their horses to the Americans, and Fort Balfour was burned to the ground.

The authorities had been waiting to get their hands on Thomas Fenwick, but hanging a British officer wasn't that easy. In the end, the militia decided to release him in a prison exchange. Thomas Fenwick had slipped the noose.

Edward Fenwick, seeing the war turning in the favor of the Americans, decided it was best to hedge his bets. Beginning sometime in 1782, he used his position as a captain in the British Army to feed the American forces intelligence about the movements and strengths of British troops. It was a shrewd move—only six weeks later the combined American and French victory over Lord Cornwallis at Yorktown effectively ended British military activity in the South and forced a negotiated peace. The thirteen colonies gained full independence, and the English evacuated Charles Town in December 1782.

As the English began their evacuation of Fenwick Hall, Thomas loaded all that he could carry or steal, including nearly three hundred slaves, and sailed to Jamaica. He would never see the plantation again. Though his name was placed on the List of Confiscated Estates, Edward Fenwick decided to stay and fight for his father's estate. General Nathaniel Greene, second only to George Washington in the American Army, wrote several letters on behalf of Edward and his property claims. Greene portrayed Fenwick as a Patriot spy serving as a captain in the British Army. An example from one letter written in Charleston in February 1785 states:

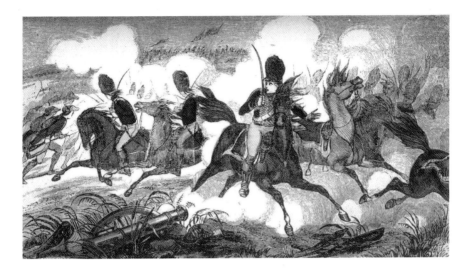

Battle of the dragoons. Frost 1860.

Intelligence to an army is like the soul to the body, it directs all its motions. To obtain this with the greatest certainty and to have an opportunity of comparing different accounts created a necessity for employing a number of persons in this service — among whom Mr. Fenwick's intelligence was accurate and seasonable. We had timely information from him to counteract several British detachments. All the Country can witness from their continual alarms how necessary this was for their safety. And when I consider how much men are disposed for war, and how many political intrigues are employed to effect it I cannot help apprehending this may be our destination at some future day.

After years of legal haggling with the government and his relatives, Edward Fenwick abandoned any hope of holding Fenwick Hall. The plantation was sold to the Gibbes family in 1788. Edward moved to lands on the South Edisto River, where he resumed the family tradition of horse breeding.

But the story of the Carolina Fenwicks was not quite over. When the British returned in the War of 1812, a descendant of the Fenwick clan served as a general for the American cause. He is widely considered one of the great heroes of that war and man of unwavering patriotism.

The Fenwicks had been redeemed.

THE MURDER OF FRANCIS DAWSON

In the annals of Southern history are many murders, some more lurid than others. However, none reads more like a dime novel than the tale of the murder of Francis Warrington Dawson. Consider the cast of characters: Francis Warrington Dawson, born Austin John Reeks, an English transplant with a storied past whose sympathies with the Confederacy brought him from England to Virginia in the hope of joining Lee's Army of the Potomac; Dr. Thomas Ballard McDow, a native of Camden and himself the son of a doctor, whose professional activities associated him with members of the black community, an irony that would stand him in good stead later; and Helene Marie Burdayron, a Swiss beauty whose presence in the Dawson house and on the streets of Charleston snared the attention of McDow, attention she later disavowed. To this mix add the Southern credo of defending one's honor and the time-honored belief that a man's home is his castle. Throw in an unhappy marriage, a victim with a number of enemies— apparently self-made—and a disinclination for the public to leave behind the antebellum South with all its attendant social and political ramifications. It was a murder waiting to happen.

Born in 1840 in London, Austin John Reeks early found himself on the fast track to nowhere. His familial ties were monied and noble; however, his father, Joseph Austin Reeks, fell on hard times through a series of spectacularly bad investments and spent the balance of his life trying to recoup both his financial and his social losses. The hapless Austin was taken under the wing of his mother's sister, the wife of Captain William A. Dawson. His aunt intended to educate the young man at Saint-Omer College in France, his father's and grandfather's alma mater. While touring Europe, Austin received word that his aunt had suffered a stroke. Returning to England to secure what he considered his inheritance, Austin unfortunately learned that he had been done out of it by grasping cousins, an act which left him with few options and little hope. Showing a creative bent that would later serve him well, Austin penned and produced several plays that were performed on the London stage. By the age of twenty, he had achieved a modicum of success and had demonstrated an ability to land on his feet.

However, all did not continue to go well. Tensions in the Reeks household grew, understandably, because the financial situation was precarious and the family was large. Austin's continuing presence in the house became a problem and resulted in a showdown between father and son. Austin's increasing interest in the cause of the Confederacy in the young nation of America was the catalyst for the final blowup between the two men. The attack on Fort Sumter solidified Austin's resolve and provided the perfect excuse for escaping what he saw was a future without hope if he stayed in England. The elder Reeks feared his son would be captured en route to the United States, thus bringing dishonor on their family. Apparently unwilling to bow to his father's will, Austin left England aboard the *Nashville* and headed for the Confederate States of America, a move that undoubtedly bolstered his self-esteem. Austin's avowed reason for joining the Southern cause was the Confederacy's stance on states' rights and self-rule, a position he could trace in his own family's history. Still known as Austin Reeks, he boarded the ship on New Year's Day in 1862, in the port of Southampton. From that point on, he would be known as Francis Warrington Dawson, the last name being a nod to an uncle who had perished in the Sepoy Mutiny. Being a good Catholic, he chose "Francis" from the famous saint of Assisi and the middle name "Warrington" from a close relative. His departure was the beginning of an adventure, the end of which no one could have foreseen.

Apparently gifted with a persuasive nature, Dawson talked his way into a job aboard the ship. Saying that he had been ordered to report, he convinced the warily skeptical Lieutenant Commander Robert Baker Pegram that he had seafaring experience. The truth was that his "experience" consisted of reading about life at sea and "sailing" miniature yachts at Hyde Park. Nevertheless, Dawson seemed to prosper. Gaining favor because of his education, he was moved to different quarters aboard the ship and took his meals with the officers. Ship's records written by Pegram, who gave him a job as a clerk and the title of master's mate, provide glowing details about Dawson's performance. It also helped his cause that he was coming to this country to serve the Confederacy. The trip across the Atlantic lasted two months and included a tour of Southern ports from Norfolk to New Orleans. In June of 1862, Dawson resigned his commission to join the Confederate army in Virginia. By the end of June, he had already seen action at Mechanicsville, Virginia, as a member of the Purcell Battery, commanded by the nephew of his former naval commander, Pegram.

Within two years, by April 1864, he had been made a captain, a testament to his abilities. Taken prisoner once and wounded several times, Dawson became a combat veteran. The life of a soldier appealed to him, as did being in the heat of battle. Those who fought with him described him as being both brave and capable. His letters to England reflect his love of the pageantry of war and the glories of battle. Surely, the entire process of battle must have appealed to his more dramatic nature. In fact, the battle of Fredericksburg was exalted by Dawson in a letter to his mother, to whom he waxed nearly poetic about his performance and the thrill of the conflict. Interestingly, it was this same battle that led General Robert E. Lee to say, "It is well that war is so terrible, else we should grow too fond of it."

Because of his polished demeanor, Dawson was a welcome addition to Virginia society. Invited to private parties both in Richmond and at plantations, fêtes attended by Virginia's finest citizens, Dawson gained a taste for the good life. However, the end of the war left Dawson without real prospects for a job. Working at a variety of trades, including that of bookkeeper and editorial assistant, Dawson realized that there was no money to be had unless he opened his own business. He was also astute enough to know that regardless of his select friends, he could not stay in Virginia successfully unless he had money. His opportunities had to lie elsewhere.

During his newspaper days in Virginia, Dawson worked and shared living quarters with Bartholomew Riordan. The friendship later proved

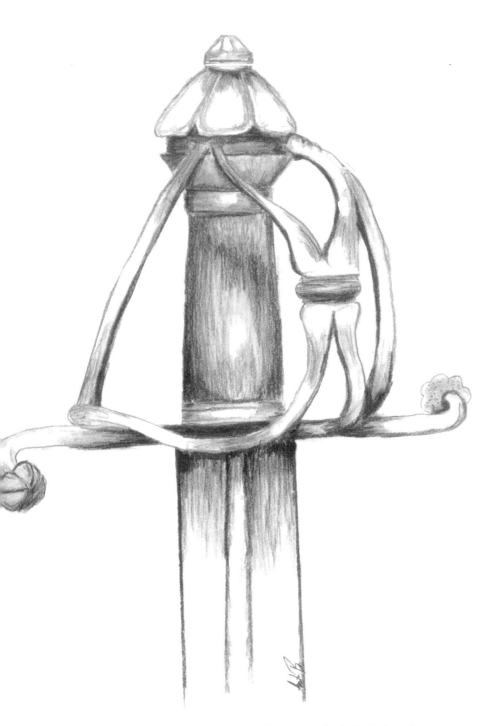

"It is well that war is so terrible, else we should grow too fond of it." *Austin Bunn*.

profitable for Dawson. The two discussed starting a cheap newspaper in Charleston, but nothing fruitful came of the talk until 1866. By that time Riordan had accepted a job at the *Charleston Courier*. There, Riordan convinced Colonel Robert Barnwell Rhett, the owner of the *Charleston Mercury*, that Dawson was what he needed to get the then-struggling *Mercury* back on its feet. Colonel Rhett wrote Dawson and offered him a job. In November of 1866, Dawson was in Charleston and immediately succumbed to the city's charms. In less than a year, Dawson was married to Virginia Fourgeaud, five years his junior, after only three months of courtship. The newlyweds lived with her family.

It soon became obvious that the *Mercury* was doomed. At times Dawson was not even paid. Never a man to be without useful connections, Dawson again landed on his feet. He and Riordan convinced the president of the South Carolina railroad to loan them six thousand dollars to purchase the struggling *News*. They also convinced Benjamin Woods of New York City to be a silent partner and to loan them the balance they needed for the purchase. The two managed to kill their competition, the *Mercury*, leaving their paper and the *Courier* as Charleston's only true sources of news. Within five years, they had become so successful that they were able to purchase the *Courier* for $7,100. By April 7, 1873, the two men were the owners and publishers of Charleston's *News and Courier*. Dawson's success was marred by the death of his wife, who had been ill with consumption, on December 6, 1872. Over the course of the next sixteen years, Dawson was often recognized for both his humanitarian work and his writing. The complexity of his relationship with the public is noted in the fact that he was respected and feared, both distinctions well earned.

Dawson established a stable family life when he married the second time. He met his new wife, Sarah Ida Fowler Morgan, while visiting an army friend, James Morris Morgan, who lived in Columbia and was recovering from a gunshot wound. Also visiting Morgan was his sister Sarah. Immediately, Dawson began to woo her. Educated in Europe and a member of Louisiana's wealthy elite, Sarah was beautiful and intelligent, as well as an accomplished scholar and talented musician. Diminutive and engaging, she fit Dawson's romantic vision; less than five feet tall, she was breathtaking, blessed with golden ringlets and blue eyes. She herself was a talented writer with an interest in all things French, which she spoke fluently. Her writing skills are evidenced in the extensive collection of letters between her and Dawson. It is likely that being both well-read and well-traveled made Sarah a suitable match for Dawson, even though her shyness contrasted with his gregariousness. She was shy to the point of reluctance to mingle with society, which in her role as the wife of one of Charleston's most prominent citizens would have been necessary.

In the midst of their courtship, Sarah's brother James married, leaving Sarah and her mother with nowhere to go. Prone to action instead of reticence, Dawson brought the pair to Charleston sometime after the summer of 1873 and ensconced them in a house he owned on Gadsden Street. He was thus both the suitor of Sarah and the provider of some of their living expenses. Dawson and Sarah married on January 27, 1874, in the Gadsden Street house, and the service was performed by Bishop Lynch, who had exhorted his parishioners to celebrate the secession of South Carolina from the Union. The pair forged a relationship in which Sarah was both Dawson's friend and his confidante. For the duration of their marriage, she was a critic of his work and gave him advice, which he often took on both his work and his politics.

Soon after their marriage, Sarah's mother died, and within a year, their first child, Ethel Morgan, was born. Their son, Francis Warrington Dawson Jr., was born on September 27, 1878, while they were living in a home on Meeting Street. The final child died in their Bull Street house (which they were occupying when Dawson was killed) at six months of age.

The Bull Street house itself was a reflection of how the Dawsons perceived themselves. Patterned after the English country houses with which Dawson would have been familiar, the house was bought after Sarah saw it and said she had to have it. The house was resplendent with carved marble fireplaces, enormous mirrors, a curved stairway that led to their bedrooms upstairs and spacious rooms, one of which could be converted into a smaller, more intimate gathering place by pulling rolling partitions and doors across it. Occasionally, Dawson worked at a desk in his bedroom upstairs in the house. At those times Sarah could be found reading in a nearby chair, from which position she could—and did—make suggestions and offer criticism of his work.

Dawson's personal regimen and appearance reflected a strict English background. He summoned servants with a bell system, bathed in cold water (though hot water was available) and dressed with all the pretentiousness of a dandy. His normal office attire included striped pants, a black cutaway coat, vest, gloves and top hat. In summer months, the top hat was replaced by a straw hat. Dawson bore the demeanor of the lord of the manor, a position bolstered by Sarah's attentions. On evenings when Dawson was late and missed dinner with the family, which was the norm, it was their custom for Sarah to wait up, dress to the nines and share a cold meal with him, over which they would often visit and talk into the early morning hours. Although Sarah was well cared for, she never enjoyed good health. She was often in pain, suffered several miscarriages and tended to be morose, a great concern for Dawson. Nevertheless, the children felt their father and mother were doting parents and that life was generally good for them.

The dark periods in an otherwise serene existence were the threats made against Dawson by unhappy newspaper readers who disagreed with his politics and the constant challenges to duels by those who felt wronged by his paper. The issue of dueling was an ever-present concern for Dawson, whose writings and influence were frequently focused on ending this Southern custom that he regarded as nothing short of barbaric. One has to wonder how Captain Dawson was really viewed by both Charlestonians and South Carolinians. The sight of him in gloves and a top hat must have provided the locals with ample cause for speculation and bemusement. He was *in* the South, but he was not *of* the South. Therein lay the source of his problems.

As the owner and editor of one of South Carolina's most powerful and widely read newspapers, Dawson was in a unique position to comment on events and sway public opinion. His views, however, often reflected more his English background than Southern traditions, showing him to be an outsider in spite of his hopes and intentions to the contrary. Intelligent, independent and intimidating, Dawson found himself at odds with the attempts of some Charlestonians to cling to their romanticized past rather than move toward the future. Dawson had full knowledge of England's move from an agrarian society to an industrialized economy. He also knew that in order to survive, the South would have to do the same. As an outsider, Dawson's position allowed him to look objectively at the situation South Carolina faced in the wake of the social, economic and cultural devastation caused by the Civil War. However, as an outsider, Dawson was also unable to relate to the intransigence of Charleston's grip on the past. Stating rather forcefully his view that the thinking of those who clung to the past was ill considered at best, Dawson caused many in Charleston to view him with some degree of consternation. But it was Dawson's lack of understanding of race relations in the South and the practice of dueling to defend one's honor that would prove to be the two contentious issues that most separated him from his fellow citizens in South Carolina.

When Dawson took over the newspaper, the biggest political issue concerned ridding the state of Yankee troops. Following Reconstruction, South Carolina was the last state from which troops were removed. The truth was that South Carolina had a ruling class and that those accustomed to ruling wanted to continue ruling. Once shed of Federal intervention, these conservative Democrats could bide their time. Among the chief proponents of this view was General Wade Hampton, who with others attempted to convince Congress that South Carolina had seen the errors of her ways and would comply with the law of the land. Martin Gary, a rather hotheaded white supremacist, espoused another position. He wanted to adopt what was known as the Mississippi Plan, or the Straight-out Plan, which blatantly advocated the use of violence to maintain white superiority by forcing blacks back into "their place." He favored intimidating blacks into staying away from the polls, thus allowing white supremacy in office and ensuring the submissive role of blacks in the state. The views held by Wade Hampton offered hope that the end of Federal occupation was near. Dawson supported this idea and wrote about it in the *News and Courier*. He gave Gary no easy way to advance his views, offering him newspaper space only at the going advertising rate to relate his stance to the public.

In 1876, South Carolina was preparing to elect a governor. Dawson, a member of the State Democratic Party Executive Committee, was enthusiastically supporting Wade Hampton with his conciliatory position of accepting the dictates of the Federal government in relation to African Americans being afforded their full Constitutional rights and freedom from fear. The *News and Courier* effectively carried the message that only with the election of a conservative Democrat to the governor's seat would Federal troops leave the state. The so-called Radical Democrats, the "straight-outs," were given no voice in Dawson's newspaper.

On the surface, it would appear that Dawson truly believed that African Americans should become functioning citizens of the state. The war was over, and it was time for South Carolinians to accept the realities of defeat. However, Wade Hampton, Dawson and a myriad of others simply saw that there were more devious means, other than blatant violence, of robbing the black man of his civil rights. There was a Republican governor to depose, and Democrats had to "fuse" the party to guarantee a victory, run the "Yankees" back home and get the blacks out of political office. Through the *News and Courier*, Dawson proved all too willing to support such methods as gerrymandering of districts and literacy tests to end suffrage for blacks in South Carolina. Hampton went on to become governor in 1876, and 1879 saw a general amnesty declared for South Carolina. To all appearances, an orderly existence had been maintained; nevertheless, Dawson's thinly veiled position of excluding blacks gained him enemies among both whites and blacks who were not fooled by his rhetoric.

By the late 1880s, Frank Dawson's business affairs were in a state of flux. An upstart journal, *The World*, was cutting into the circulation of the *News and Courier*. Several of Dawson's best reporters and journalists had gone over to the competition. These desertions put even more pressure on Dawson to produce the best newspaper in the state. Complicating the situation was the fact that *The World* was the mouthpiece for the Tillman movement and for those who wanted to provide a forum for the "up-towners" tired of the Charleston "ring" propaganda. The competition saw itself as not just for subscribers but also for the hearts and minds of South Carolinians. The editorial attacks were most often personal diatribes against Dawson who, so the articles claimed, represented the aristocratic "dandies" who strangled any hope for the political empowerment of the common people of the state.

Dawson, who in the best of times was demanding and highly critical of his employees' work, now became almost imperial in his attitudes concerning what was expected of his staff. He was even more merciless regarding his own efforts to keep the newspaper ahead of any competition, and his health was beginning to show the effects of his stress. To add to Dawson's woes, he was having difficulty raising the money to keep the *News and Courier* afloat. In the early months of 1889, he went to New York expecting to procure the necessary loans to take his newspaper through the current hard times. Instead, he came home with no money and a life insurance policy for only $2,500. Dawson had wanted to financially protect his wife and children with something more substantial than this pauperish amount. However, his bouts with stomach ulcers and his portly appearance did not make him a very good investment. Nevertheless, upon returning to Charleston, Dawson optimistically assured his wife that the present setbacks were only temporary. It soon became obvious, however, that Dawson's situation was fraught with stress on every level. It is no wonder that his life took a downward—and fatal—turn, as Dawson soon found himself in conflict with a neighboring doctor and the black community he served.

Thomas Ballard McDow was a true son of the South, born in Camden, South Carolina, and the son of a doctor who practiced in Lancaster. Educated at Cumberland University in Tennessee, he went on to graduate as the valedictorian of his class at the Medical College of Charleston. Although little is known of his early years after college, it is known that he was involved in a shooting incident in Mississippi and enjoyed a reputation for having a bad temper. His medical clientele was largely made up of blacks, which during his trial for Dawson's murder worked to his advantage. Rumors in Charleston hinted that McDow performed abortions among the blacks and also signed fraudulent death certificates that allowed blacks to collect death benefits. It was further rumored that he took drugs. Because of the rumors concerning his unethical professional activities and his perceived substance abuse, McDow was unofficially blackballed by the medical community, which regarded him as a persona non grata. Add to this the fact that he was unhappily married to a German woman of some financial means. Handsome and dark-haired, McDow was of slight build, a sharp contrast with his more substantial wife, who in those days would have been referred to as "stout," and also with Dawson, who was considerably larger in both height and weight. McDow's personal unhappiness undoubtedly contributed to his fascination with the beautiful, young and voluptuous Helene Marie Burdayron, the governess for the Dawson children. When his attentions toward Helene became known to Dawson, a series of events was set into motion that doomed Dawson and led to a sensational trial that rocked Charleston and much of South Carolina.

The background of the woman whose presence was the catalyst for the death of Frank Dawson and the trial of McDow is sketchy at best. Helene Burdayron was brought to Charleston specifically to serve as the governess for the Dawson children. Because of her youth, Dawson had promised to act as her guardian and protector. After Dawson's death, unsubstantiated rumors circulated that he had had an affair with Helene; and there is evidence that she was not wholly innocent in some ways. Beautiful and foreign, she was perceived by many in the city as a seductress. It is also likely that being foreign, she was not aware of the constraints of Southern society and the proprieties required of Southern ladies. The exact nature of the communications between McDow and Helene is unknown; however, she did give him a book titled *Twixt Love and Law*, the story of an illicit affair between a married man and an unmarried woman. The nature of the book caused a stir and contributed to the public perception of Helene as a temptress. The pair was reportedly seen walking about together and riding different trolleys to meeting points distant from where they were living so they could secretly see each other.

It is probable that Helene meant nothing other than a harmless flirtation with the handsome doctor and that her youth contributed to McDow's misunderstanding her intentions. Nevertheless, the relationship was not seen as such by Dawson, who had been told that his governess had been seen around town with an unsavory companion. Dawson went to Charleston's police chief, Joseph Golden, and requested that he investigate the matter. Golden had Helene followed and reported to Dawson at the offices of the *News and Courier* that his governess had been seen in the company of McDow for quite some time and that the pair had taken circuitous routes to their meeting place. Dawson vowed that he would handle it on his way home from work. Golden knew McDow, and warned Dawson not to approach him because of the doctor's poor reputation. Dawson ignored Golden's advice, left work early and went to McDow's home office to confront him with the information he had. As he rode the trolley to McDow's office, Dawson did not appear agitated or upset. In fact, his manner was rather congenial. However, matters quickly got out of hand once he entered McDow's office. It was there that Dawson lost his life on March 12, 1889.

More than likely, Dawson did not intend to stay at McDow's office for very long. When his body was found, he was still wearing his gloves and coat. Witnesses at the trial reported seeing and hearing some of what transpired between the two men. One black man, George W. Harper, later testified that he was waiting in his carriage for passengers to come out of their house when he heard shots, sounds of some sort of struggle and groans coming from the doctor's office. Harper also reported hearing a voice saying, in essence, "You have taken my life" shortly prior to the basement office window's being abruptly closed by the doctor. Almost immediately, another person on the street, a woman who sold nut cakes, peered in the window and said that someone had been murdered inside. What followed was a flurry of activity. The doctor went to the second-floor piazza and looked around the area. McDow's butler hitched up the doctor's carriage, in which his wife and child quickly left.

Harper's passengers finally came out and entered his carriage. As he drove them past the policeman who had been stationed at the corner as a precaution by Chief Golden, Harper related to the officer that someone had been killed in the doctor's office. The policeman went to McDow's office and inquired about what had happened. McDow peeped out and reassured the officer that nothing was amiss, yet the officer went to Golden and reported what he had been told. Golden visited McDow's office himself and was told the same thing by McDow. Unconvinced, Golden went to the *News and Courier* office and was told that Dawson had left early. In checking with Dawson's wife, Golden learned that the publisher had not arrived home. Alarmed, Golden next went to the mayor's office for a warrant. In the interim, some three hours after Dawson's death, McDow went to the police station and turned himself in, admitting openly that he had killed Dawson. He further stated that he had meant to kill him and believed he had done so as an act of self-defense. Meanwhile, Sarah Dawson, who for hours had frantically awaited word of her husband, was eventually told of his death. A reporter named Henry Baynard visited the house and was unable initially to tell her what had happened. Distraught, he slumped into a chair and wept, leaving her to surmise that Dawson was dead. News of the death swept through the city the next day, carried on the pages of the *News and Courier* Dawson had led for so many years.

During the initial investigation, many details about what had happened came to light. An examination of Dawson's body and clothing revealed several interesting facts. The fatal wound was a gunshot in the back, the bullet fired apparently from some distance because no gunpowder burns or residue were found. Dr. William Middleton Michel performed the autopsy and found that death had occurred because of the path of the bullet, which traversed the abdomen, went through the right kidney and nicked the vena cava, causing internal bleeding and almost instantaneous death. The examination also revealed that there was a lack of powder burns, which meant that Dawson was not shot at close range. Since McDow was the only witness to the killing, it was difficult to determine, given the forensics of the day, the precise circumstances and the events that had precipitated the shooting. On at least one critical point, McDow himself provided conflicting evidence.

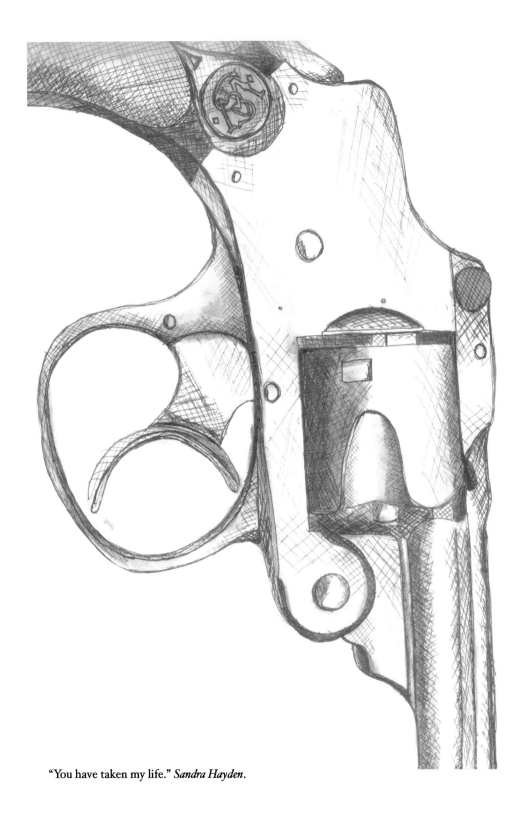

"You have taken my life." *Sandra Hayden.*

According to McDow, Dawson had come to his office and confronted him about his relationship with Helene Marie Burdayron and what Dawson considered McDow's unseemly behavior toward her. McDow denied the matter, but Dawson insisted that McDow give up seeing the young woman or risk exposure in the newspaper. McDow told Dawson he would hold him personally responsible if he did so and ordered the much larger Dawson out of his office. McDow claimed that Dawson struck him on the head with his cane, pushed him backward onto a sofa and was advancing again when McDow pulled out a gun from his desk and fatally shot him. In contradictory testimony, under oath, McDow later stated that the gun came from his trouser pocket. But he never denied that he had killed Dawson.

In a remarkable admission on the stand, McDow recounted how he had tried to cover up his crime. At one point he had tried to shove the body underneath a stairway, as evidenced by the dirt on Dawson's body as well as the whitewash that covered both men's clothing. He thought better of that course of action and dragged the body back out into the office, attempting to clean it up to hide his earlier actions. Sometime during the three-hour interval between the murder and his turning himself in at police headquarters, McDow also visited the Dawson home, which was just around the corner from McDow's home, apparently to tell Helene Burdayron what had happened. When Sarah Dawson herself answered the door, McDow, whom she did not know, left. Throughout the testimony, McDow never denied that he had shot Dawson and steadfastly maintained that he had felt threatened physically by Dawson and had acted only in self-defense. After all, it was both his home and office that had been invaded by the furious Dawson. It is interesting to note that McDow, upon examination at the police station, bore no signs of having been struck on the head as he alleged Dawson had done.

Captain Francis Dawson was laid to rest amidst pomp and accolades usually reserved for heads of state. Mourners and flowers overflowed the Catholic church that Dawson had attended. Businesses were closed as throngs of bereaved Charlestonians lined the streets and wept as the funeral cortege slowly passed on its way to the Catholic Cemetery of Saint Lawrence. As the summer approached, the sensational story of Dawson's death waned. However, the trial of Dr. Thomas McDow promised to break the monotony of the steamy Charleston summer. Especially titillating was the prospect of seeing the beautiful Helene

Burdayron on the stand. What would she say to affirm or deny the rumors of an illicit relationship with her employer's killer?

The Honorable Joseph Brevard Kershaw called to order the General Sessions Court of Charleston. The courtroom overflowed with spectators, many of whom were blacks supporting Dr. McDow. The legal adversaries in this trial were among the most notable jurists in the state. Judge Andrew Gordon and Mr. Asher D. Cohen represented the defendant while the prosecution was made up of the First Circuit Solicitor Mr. William St. Julien Jervey and Mr. Henry Augustus Middleton Smith. The jury comprised seven blacks and five whites. Curiously, this seems to have been the first time that a majority of blacks had been chosen to serve on the jury for a trial of such magnitude. The stage was set for quite a show.

Miss Burdayron, age twenty-two, took the stand on the second day of the trial. There was a hush over the entire courtroom as the voluptuous young woman came forward to be sworn in. Dressed demurely in a black dress with white lace sleeves, Miss Burdayron kept her eyes down most of the time she was on the stand. Wisps of dark hair peeped from beneath her black hat. Since Miss Burdayron's native tongue was French, she requested an interpreter, but the request was denied. From the beginning of the questioning, the young woman was composed and answered questions in an open and candid manner. Yes, she knew Dr. McDow, having met him several months prior to Captain Dawson's death. She felt great sympathy for the doctor because he was in a miserable and loveless marriage. From the beginning, McDow had implored her to run away with him. Miss Burdayron had secretly met with the doctor on many occasions. She further acknowledged that sometimes they met and walked together and that at other times, when the Dawsons were away, he came to their home. McDow and Burdayron had exchanged gifts, and she conceded that one of her gifts had been the book *Twixt Love and Law*. However, she claimed profusely that merely giving him that book did not insinuate that her relationship with the doctor was similar to the story in the book, which told of a young unmarried girl's affair with a married man. At one point she admitted that McDow had kissed her but that she had neither wanted nor encouraged that to happen. The defense implied through questions in the cross-examination that she, not he, was the seducer. However, her calm and naive manner seemed to dispel any impression that such was the case.

When the prosecution had finished presenting its evidence, the defense began to make its case. On the third day of the trial, McDow took the stand. Under questioning by his attorney, McDow was asked about the manner in which Dawson had entered his office. McDow presented a picture of an enraged Dawson who had threatened him both physically and verbally. McDow feared that Dawson meant him harm and that his life was in danger because Dawson had struck him with his cane. When asked if Dawson had confronted him, McDow said that he had and gave the impression that Dawson was in front of him with his cane raised and was preparing to strike him again. McDow was also forced to review how he had tried to conceal the body, but he remained impressively calm throughout the retelling of the grim details. Despite the two hours of testifying, McDow remained composed and impassive.

The defense also called to the stand a medical expert to give an alternative explanation as to how Captain Dawson had died. There was no doubt, of course, as to how he died and by whose hands. But the key question was whether or not Dr. McDow's statements concerning the sequence of events leading to Dawson's death were credible. Defense attorney Mr. Asher Cohen, noted for his skill in cross-examining witnesses, called the defense's medical expert to give his opinion on the trajectory of the bullet. In his opinion, the bullet could have traveled from the side and the front. Understanding what the defense was trying to imply through their medical expert's findings, the prosecution called a second medical expert, a faculty member from the Medical College of South Carolina, to the stand. In his testimony, the witness stated that Dr. Michel was remiss in not verifying the final lodgment of the bullet and suggested, contrary to Dr. Michel's medical opinions, that something other than bone could deflect a bullet's path through the body. Dr. Michel was recalled to the stand where he reiterated his previous opinion that only bone could impede the movement of a bullet through a body. It was apparent to all in the courtroom that Cohen had skillfully maneuvered the doctor into impugning the medical expertise of the professor of clinical surgery at the Medical College of South Carolina. Cohen had accomplished his goal of planting in the jurors' minds that there was more than one possible explanation of how Dawson had been killed. The worst scenario was dispelled because the evidence did not conclusively prove that Dawson had been shot in the back as he attempted to leave the doctor's office. However, the defense still lacked an explanation for the absence of the powder burns that should have been on Dawson's body had he been shot at close range. Nevertheless, the jury and, in large parts, the public ultimately chose to ignore that pertinent evidence.

The balance of the defense's strategy involved trying to prove several points. One was that police chief Golden had apparently considered Dawson to be angry and dangerous because he otherwise would not have stationed a special officer near the McDow home. Furthermore, witnesses, some known to be Dawson's enemies, also vouched that Dawson was prone to violent verbal outbursts and had the potential for being physically abusive as well. Carriage driver Harper remained unshaken in his assertion that he had heard McDow shout that Dawson had tried to kill him but that he had gotten him first. The most salient point, however, was the defense's contention that the murder had occurred in McDow's home, which Dawson had entered in a threatening manner—that a man's home was his castle, and that he had a right to defend it.

At the close of the trial, defense attorney Cohen requested that the presiding judge remind the jury of several points of law concerning murder. Among the points explained to the jury were that murder differs from self-defense primarily in intent and that murder involves malice aforethought. The jurors were also reminded that a man's office could be considered his home and would thereby mean he was afforded the same right to defend his office as he was his home. Furthermore, a man was under no obligation to retreat in his home and if he asked a visitor to leave, said visitor was compelled to do so. Finally, they were reminded that they had to find McDow guilty beyond a reasonable doubt.

Naturally, the summations of the opposing attorneys to the jury differed greatly. On Friday both Cohen and McGrath addressed the jury. Cohen spoke for nearly three hours and laid the foundation for his colleague's presentation, portraying his client as suffering greatly over the incident. Judge McGrath, an attorney of solid repute, reviewed the facts as he saw them and reminded the jurors of their duty. In a stroke of genius, he offered his sympathies to those who were deciding his client's fate, saying that they had been left with insufficient light on a terrible case and that only the presence of the carriage driver had given them the power to save McDow. On Saturday morning Prosecutor Mitchell drew a picture of Dawson as a gregarious man in a splendid mood on the afternoon of his murder. He reviewed details such as the lack of an apparent injury on McDow, thereby calling into question McDow's contention that Dawson had struck him, and reminded the jury that McDow had contradicted himself in the matter of the gun and whether it was in a desk or on his person. Surely, they could not believe a man who told conflicting tales. Mitchell also reminded them that no powder burns were found on Dawson's body, meaning that the shooting had to have been from some distance and that therefore McDow could not have been too threatened. Mitchell had the good sense not to attack Miss Burdayron, saying in essence that she too was a victim and had been seduced by McDow, reasoning that men had stronger passions than women and that women's passions paled by contrast.

The jury retired around noon on that Saturday after listening to six days of testimony. For less than three hours, the jury deliberated, asking only once for evidence, a diagram of the scene of the murder. By mid-afternoon, a not-guilty verdict had been reached. What is most obvious is that the victim was on trial at least as much as the defendant. The composition of the jury provides a clue regarding the outcome. The black jurors had probably favored McDow because of his history of sympathetic treatment of the black community. They had also doubtlessly recalled Dawson's published positions favoring the treatment of whites over blacks. Of the white jurors, one was a known political enemy of Dawson who could easily have swayed the remainder of the whites on the jury. And after all, Dawson was a foreigner who had lived among their community but who had never understood the South's complicated codes of honor and conduct.

SAVED BY GRACE ALONE

F ew murder cases in Charleston history have inspired the same bewilderment as that of the 1935 murder of Frances Craven. The story is tragic, underscored by the curious manner in which the killer was treated after his capture. The details of the murder are unchallenged: a jilted lover used a .32-caliber pistol to shoot his girlfriend at point-blank range, while her children watched. The suspect confessed and provided authorities with his motive: Craven had rejected him. In a perfect world, this would have been an open-and-shut case. But in Charleston, there would be no justice for Frances Craven.

Beginning the very day of his arrest, Eugene Pop enjoyed a level of compassion and kindness generally reserved for the victim of a crime, not a confessed killer. He was suddenly transformed in the public's perception from adulterer and drunk to "avenging angel," the victim of both a cruel society and a "wicked woman." This image was carefully cultivated by defense attorney John P. Grace, one-time mayor of Charleston, and quickly accepted and promoted by Charleston's more sanctimonious residents, who fiercely defended Pop through his incarceration and trial for the murder of Craven.

Frances Craven was a mother of three who had been widowed during the height of the Great Depression. She was well liked and had an easy-going attitude that matched her beautiful smile. But she was a single mother living on the wrong side of the tracks, and would have been looked down upon as little more than white trash by many people in Charleston.

Frances was like a lot of people in the Great Depression. She was unsure of her future, but determined to take care of her children. She worked a full-time job, and to make ends meet she took boarders at her house at 59 Charlotte Street. Eugene Pop was born in Charleston in an area commonly referred to as the Borough. He was the son of a blue-collar father who became crippled when Eugene was still a boy. Forced into the role of family breadwinner at age ten, Pop never had a childhood. When the Great Depression hit Charleston, he moved from job to job before finding steady work at the navy yard. He married, paid his bills on time and stayed out of trouble. By all accounts, he was a model citizen.

Craven and Pop met in November 1929 when Frances was having work done on her home and Eugene was moonlighting as an electrician. There was an instant attraction. Though she was recently widowed and he was married, the couple was seen everywhere together. They went to the movies, attended parties, ate meals and danced together. Pop soon became the man of the house, taking charge of keeping it up and dealing with the boarders who came through.

Eventually, things started going downhill. Eugene took up drinking with a real commitment. Whatever discipline or industry had sustained him through his tough childhood was abandoned and he became an ornery, lazy, shiftless drunk. Frances began leaving the children at home alone, sometimes not showing up until the next day and usually reeking of alcohol. She became easily agitated and flew into rages over Eugene's rumored infidelities. Eugene turned drinking into a steady profession, and was altogether belligerent when he bothered to show up at the Craven house at all.

Fearful of Eugene, Frances's children, Daisy, Violet and Bobby, told their mother that she had to make a choice between her family and her boyfriend. They were vehement in their disapproval of Eugene Pop and their desire for their mother to end the romance permanently. In fact, Frances had already decided to end the relationship, but it was proving more difficult than she imagined. She knew that he would take it hard. In the end, Frances chose to avoid him. For Eugene, that may have been worse than outright rejection—he immediately assumed she was off with other men.

For weeks, Eugene turned up at the house threatening anyone who would listen. He dwelled on Frances for hours each day and seethed at the prospect of being rejected. He neglected his work and began to drink in local bars where he sat alone and wallowed in self-pity. Always paranoid about being left for another man, Eugene could feel himself losing control of Frances, and he knew it would only be a matter of time before she left him completely. After days of waiting to hear from her, his worst fears were realized. Frances told him that it was over and that he was never to return to her house again.

Eugene flew into a rage, showing up at the house and cursing the oldest daughter, Daisy. Daisy called the police, who removed Eugene from the house and ordered him to stay away. Eugene felt betrayed and humiliated. He had given Frances money and six years of his life. She spurned him and then had the nerve to have him arrested. He was convinced that Frances was seeing someone else, a possibility that tore at his pride and ate at his thoughts. He resolved to avenge this terrible insult.

On November 9, 1935, the Craven family ate dinner together, and then Daisy and Frances went to the kitchen to wash the dishes. About that time, Eugene Pop staggered through the front door and began cursing and threatening Frances. When she ordered him to leave, Eugene pulled a pistol and fired. His first shot went high and a terrible struggle ensued as Frances tried to pry the gun from his hands. As they wrestled for the weapon, Bobby and Violet heard the ruckus and rushed to their mother's defense. Ten-year-old Bobby caught Eugene squarely in the head with a fruit jar, causing a gash and sending blood running squarely down his face. Just as Daisy jumped in to get the gun away from Eugene, he broke free and Frances was knocked to the floor. Pleading for her life, she instinctively turned her face, in anticipation of the shot. Without hesitation, Pop raised the pistol and shot her in the head. Blood splattered the walls of the room. He then wheeled violently to his left and shot Daisy Craven at point-blank range.

In a state of panic, and positive that the entire neighborhood had heard the commotion, Pop ran from the house. He paused briefly when he saw a neighbor stepping into the street to see what the fuss was about. Another neighbor, Mr. Altine, grabbed his own gun and pursued Pop into the darkness.

Pop ran down Elizabeth Street and entered Stevens Grocery at the corner of Elizabeth and Charlotte Streets, a short distance from the Craven home. "This guy Pop rushes in the front door, all bloody on the head, and he says, 'Steve, I've done a good job up the street.' Then he dashes out down Elizabeth Street and turns into Henrietta," E.W. Stevens later recalled in

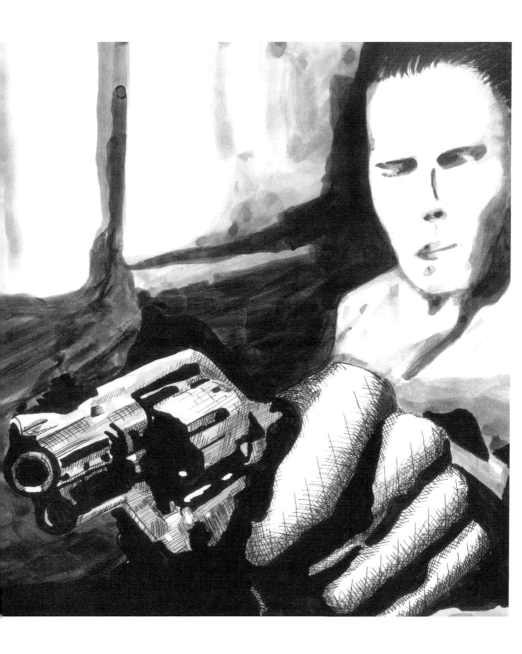

The murder. *Nick Hendrix*.

court. Pop raced up the deserted street and broke into the old Citadel barracks at Marion Square. He later said that he thought of putting a bullet into his own brain, but for whatever reason, he did not take his own life.

By 6:30 p.m., the police had received reports that an armed man was hiding in the old Citadel barracks and that he was suspected of killing a woman on Charlotte Street. The police found Pop lying face down on the second floor of the building. According to the testimony of Detective W.H. Poole, "He sat up and asked if I wanted the gun. Then he reached to his back and handed me the pistol. It was a thirty-two revolver with three loaded shells, one empty shell and two empty chambers."

Eugene Pop was arrested and transported to the Charleston jail. While in custody, he was interviewed by the coroner, Dr. DeVeaux. DeVeaux later told the jury, "He told me he had shot Mrs. Craven and Mrs. Craven's daughter and hoped he had made a damn good job of it." While Pop was bragging about how he had killed Frances Craven, Charleston detectives arrived at the murder scene and found Daisy standing on the front porch. She suffered terrible injuries, but was still alive. The gunshot had only grazed her face. She led the detectives to the kitchen where they found Frances lying face down in a pool of blood. As far as they were concerned, the case was closed.

But Pop's story made a very favorable impression on a few important men in Charleston. John P. Grace agreed to take on his defense at the request of Pop's invalid father, a man Grace knew from when he too was a Borough kid. As mayor, Grace had fought for the people—the poor, north-of-Broad, working-class people. His enemies were the so-called Bourbons, the wealthy, South-of-Broad folks that had ruled Charleston for centuries. Grace was an impressive politician, and an impressive defense attorney. He championed Eugene Pop, and thus began soliciting the public outpouring of sympathy for the man who murdered his lover and shot her daughter while they washed dishes in their own home. Many Charlestonians were all too happy to accept Grace's propaganda—Frances Craven was a woman, and her lifestyle offended the sensibilities of proper society.

The trial of Eugene Pop began in June 1936. In his opening statement, prosecutor Bob Figg reminded the jury that Pop knew he was going to kill Frances and that the murder had been premeditated. According to Figg, it was planned, it was cold and it was calculated.

When Bobby Craven took the stand, he was asked to describe the awful night when he saw his mother murdered:

Right after dinner I stayed in the dining room to play with some bows and arrows. The boy next door gave them to me. All of a sudden Pop came in the house, kind of walking fast. He went right past me but he didn't speak, he just went on through the swinging door in the kitchen.

Unflustered by the questioning, Bobby continued:

Then I heard a noise like a shot, so I yelled for Daisy and Violet. When I got out to the kitchen I saw mother trying to take a gun from Pop and she said, "Hit him, Bobby." So I picked up this fly-driver can and cracked him on the head. He didn't let go so I threw a fruit jar at him. Then Daisy was there trying to get the gun, too. But Pop got it. He shot mother down the back then he fired in Daisy's face. When he ran out the front door I grabbed an ice pick and followed him. But he got away.

In court, John Grace often portrayed Pop as a remorseful and confused man, claiming that his client was temporarily insane at the time of the assault, driven to the brink of madness by a sinful woman. While questioning Daisy Craven, he changed course, asking the teenage girl, "Daisy, are you sure your mother and Mr. Pop were struggling over a gun? Weren't they perhaps struggling in some more intimate and primitive embrace?" Daisy angrily called Grace a liar—exactly the disrespectful outburst the attorney was looking for. Each question directed at Daisy invariably led back to the issue of sex. Grace had to prove that Frances Craven was a home wrecker that needed killing.

Speaking quietly and carefully, Eugene Pop took the witness stand in the Charleston court to admit to killing Frances Craven. Grace wanted the jury to hear Pop's explanation of how and why he did it. It was important for the defense to let the court see the troubled man on the stand. Maybe they could understand that Eugene was a good man, inspired to murder by a higher cause. When Grace asked his client if he knew Mrs. Frances Craven, Pop looked straight ahead and confidently replied: "Yes, I did."

Eugene went on to describe his relationship with Frances. He told the court of their ups and downs and how they fought from time to time. Gently guided by Grace's questions, Pop painted Frances in the most unflattering light, deftly inserting accusations into his testimony

101

that she had provided nude pictures of herself for his enjoyment—a scandalous accusation in 1936. When questioned about the night of the murder, Pop claimed that Frances had invited him to the Craven home to return the nude pictures. "Frances told me to come. She said to come about three-thirty when nobody else would be home. She wanted me to bring back this picture of her."

According to Pops, it was a trap. "She was standing at the door watching for me and she pulled me inside and back to the kitchen where it was dark. She had blankets pinned up over windows. She put her arms around me and said she wanted to make up. Then this Daisy walked in and hit me over the head with a bottle and said 'You've walked into the trap at last.' So I pulled my gun."

Now trapped in the dark kitchen, Pop claimed that an unknown number of assailants began to attack from all sides. Then he made the most outrageous claim of all: "All these people were hitting me and Frances was trying to point the gun at herself, but I stopped her. I told them to get out of the way because I was going to fire in the air for help. So then I fired a couple of times and ran out of the house."

But prosecutor Figg was unmoved. During a brief but intense cross-examination, he wasted no time in shredding Pop's story to pieces. His first order of business was to discredit the story about the pornographic pictures. Handing Pop a photograph, Figg asked, "Is that a nude picture of Mrs. Craven?"

Pop considered the photograph for a moment, and lamely replied, "I don't know what you mean."

Figg continued, "In other words, you don't know what a nude picture is? You don't know a nude picture from a portrait photograph. You are just making up lies about a dead woman, a woman you say you loved, knowing that she isn't here to answer those lies."

The prosecutor continued to destroy Pop's testimony, systematically pointing out holes in his story, but the defendant never wavered. At one point he even looked to the gallery and waved to an old acquaintance. Pop had no doubt come to believe the lies he had told so many times. Besides, he had Grace on his side.

On June 10, 1936, John Grace gave his final statement to the jury. He emphasized that the defendant had been under the spell of a wicked woman, unable to determine the difference between right and wrong.

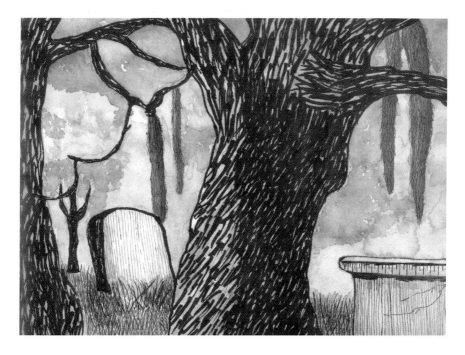

Charleston cemetery. *Holly Gleaton.*

This creature, this Mrs. Craven, not only drained him of his money but she filled his mind with sinfulness and stole his soul away. She stole him from his bride, from his friends, from his family. Then when she had used him up, this good and charitable son of good and charitable parents, she cast him out into the street.

Who was this wicked woman, this Jezebel? She said her husband was dead. Or did he leave her, unable to bear the sin and degradation of living with her any longer? What became of all the other men with whom she filled her dark days and dark nights?

You all know that Hell hath no furry like a woman scorned. Or even like a woman who thinks she is scorned. The jealous rage of this Mrs. Craven, who cast out her lover and yet burned with hatred to think that she might have a rival, caused her to set a trap for this man and to bait that trap her own body. That body on which she placed a price, even though it had no value.

Put yourselves in the place of that poor wretch in that dark room. Cajoled and then assaulted, set upon by a horde that would beat him within an inch of his life, and perhaps out of it. In terror of death or serious bodily harm, he protected himself, as any of you would do. The accidental killing that resulted from his self-defense cannot be called murder.

He sits here today, in danger of his life, through no fault of his own. To some of you it may seem that he has led a misspent life; but it has not been a malicious one. He has been led astray.

Here in this very city of Charleston there are criminals who have been indicted and have not yet been tried. Their friends are too many. There are others guilty of the larceny of thousands of dollars of public money who have been given only a slap on the wrist. Their friends are too high. And among those high and mighty there are men who planned and carried out the ruin and impoverishment of hundreds and thousands of people. Those are the cries which are premeditated. Those are the crimes of the Bourbons that go unpunished.

This poor man, friendless and forsaken by all except his humble family, is more to be pitied than censured. He is guilty of no crime except that of destroying sin. He is Eugene Pop, the avenging angel of God who wrought God's will!

The closing arguments finished, Judge Grimball instructed the jury panel to find the defendant guilty or not guilty, or guilty of manslaughter in the first degree. It took the jury little more than two hours of deliberation to reach a decision. At 7:50 p.m., the all-male jury filed into the courtroom of the Charleston County Courthouse. Frances Craven's children sat quietly at their seats. The prosecutor and defense gathered at their tables, and Judge Grimball asked the jury for their verdict. "How do you find Eugene Pop under the first count, murder in the second degree?" he asked.

"Not guilty your honor," said the jury spokesperson. On the next count, manslaughter, the jury found Eugene Pop guilty. Grace smiled. Murder meant twenty-five years to life in prison. On a manslaughter charge, Pop faced as little as one year in jail, with a maximum sentence of twenty-five years.

On June 11, 1936, Pop was brought back to court for sentencing. Judge Grimball gave him the maximum sentence under the law: twenty-five years in the penitentiary. He would be eligible for parole in just eight years. But he wouldn't serve even half that time. On January 13, 1939, less than three years after being sentenced, Eugene Pop was paroled by Governor Olin Johnston, and in 1943, he was granted a full pardon.

THE REDNECK
CHARLES MANSON

H e was a cold-blooded, vicious killer, a child rapist, a man so mean that some folks claimed that rattlesnakes wouldn't go near him. His name was Donald Henry "Pee Wee" Gaskins, one of America's most prolific, unrepentant serial killers. Embittered by years of torture, beatings and sexual abuse both in and out of prison, Gaskins evolved into the personification of evil. Most of his murderous life was spent behind bars where, despite his small stature—he stood only five foot two and weighed 130 pounds—he became the most feared man in the South Carolina correctional system.

When he was free, Gaskins stole, murdered, raped and burned his way across South Carolina in a spree of criminality that was unlike anything law enforcement had ever seen before. His favored prey were the runaways and hitchhikers he picked up while prowling South Carolina's coastal highways. But he wasn't adverse to murdering acquaintances, friends and relatives, either. Murder was therapeutic for Pee Wee. His victims hadn't caused his pain, but their torture served as the means by which he eased it. But Gaskins's murderous career will always remain somewhat of a mystery. Even up to the day he was executed, he lied with a pervasiveness that was legendary.

Donald Gaskins was born on March 13, 1933, on a dirt farm in the town of Prospect, South Carolina. Born illegitimate, Gaskins was known as "Junior Parrott" until the age of eleven, when he learned who his father was. Though his diminutive stature earned him the nickname "Pee Wee," he compensated for this shortcoming with a violent personality and a tendency to carry knives and blackjacks. When he wasn't fighting, he could be found "corn holing" local boys or stealing from his neighbors. As the *Columbia Record* later reported, "Junior always was a little different."

By age eleven, Gaskins had left school to team up with a couple of teenage hoodlums to burglarize homes and steal cars. "The Trouble Trio," as the gang called themselves, used the proceeds from their criminal activities to purchase a car and travel to Charleston and Columbia to find prostitutes. Unsatisfied with consensual sex, they brutally gang raped one of the boys' younger sisters. The boys were quickly found out by the girl's family, who strung them up by the wrists and mercilessly beat them with wooden planks and thick leather straps.

This early lesson did nothing to change Pee Wee's vile ways. Shortly after the beating, Gaskins was surprised by a cousin while burglarizing her home. After a scuffle, Pee Wee beat the girl with a blackjack, struck her over the head with a hatchet and threw her in a ditch. He was later arrested for the crime and sent to the South Carolina Industrial School for Boys until his eighteenth birthday.

Located a few miles outside Florence, the reformatory was little better than a gladiator academy. There was little or no outside supervision, a condition that promoted or at least allowed a level of abuse that is unimaginable today. A boy as young and small as Gaskins was easy prey. Only two days after he arrived, he was gang raped in a shower by more than twenty boys. To avoid the relentless sexual assaults, he eventually accepted the protection of the strongest boy in the reformatory. For this "protection" Pee Wee was doled out to other boys for sexual favors.

Repeatedly sodomized and physically tortured during his six years at the juvenile home, Gaskins decided that escape would be the best solution to his problems. He fled no less than four times from the reformatory, and returned each time to severe whippings and physical labor. On his last escape, Gaskins joined a traveling carnival working in Florida. It was there that he met his first wife, a thirteen-year-old member of the crew. After one night together as man and wife, Pee Wee decided to return to South Carolina to serve out his term at the boys' home. Upon his return, he was sentenced to solitary confinement. Isolated from human interaction, his mental problems grew extreme. In 1950, the head of the reformatory wrote about Gaskins: "We consider him dangerous and also believe that he has the homicidal tendencies peculiar to a paranoid type. We are requesting psychiatric treatment and also requesting proper placement in view of the fact that we have been unable to adjust this boy to our group."

Soon thereafter, Pee Wee was shipped off to the state mental hospital to receive treatment for his increasingly psychotic behavior. It didn't work. By the time he was released, any semblance of hope that he may have had to grow into a mature, productive adult citizen was effectively shattered. Years of abuse and physical torture had taken their toll. He bitterly called his time at the South Carolina Industrial School his "real education."

Now unleashed on the world, Gaskins resumed his life of crime, making a steady profession of burning tobacco barns and working with the owners to get the insurance money. When a young girl made the mistake of teasing him about the scams—which were the worst-kept secrets in Prospect—Gaskins nearly beat her to death with a hammer. He was arrested for assault with a deadly weapon, attempted murder and arson. Sentenced to six years, Pee Wee Gaskins entered the South Carolina state prison in the fall of 1952. It was here that he would commit his first murder.

His hands shackled and his legs bound firmly with irons, Gaskins entered into the gloomy confines of the South Carolina State Penitentiary for the first time. Though the details of the prison scene may have been unfamiliar, Pee Wee nonetheless instinctively recognized it from his time in the reformatory. He again suffered numerous rapes and soon became desperate to become a "Power Man," a boss of sorts in jail. But the only way to become a Power Man was to kill another inmate. Gaskins set his sights on Hazel Brazell, a swaggering monster that ruled the penitentiary by fear and favor. Pee Wee wasn't discouraged by Brazell's fearsome reputation. After weeks of buttering-up Brazell with gifts of money and food, Gaskins found himself alone with the most powerful man in the prison. He didn't hesitate. As Brazell sat on his toilet, Pee Wee lunged forward and buried a shank into his throat. "I didn't really feel nothing much at all," Gaskins later recalled. He was surprised to discover that killing someone was no big thing, nothing to lose sleep over. Though the killing added another three years to his sentence, to Pee Wee it was worth every day. The act gave him full run of the prison.

In 1955, Pee Wee was notified that his wife was filing for divorce. Day by day, Gaskins grew bitter and angry, consumed by his "bothersome feelings" and waiting for the day he would roam free again. His chance came when he was assigned to an outside work detail. He escaped and fled to Florida to join the carnival at Lake Wales. It was there that Pee Wee met his next wife, a young high school dropout. Barely two weeks later, he dropped her off at her parents' house and headed toward Tennessee with a voluptuous side show contortionist named Bettie Gates. When the police broke down the door of their hotel room, Pee Wee realized that he'd been duped. Bettie was already married and had used Pee Wee to aid in the escape of her husband, claiming he was actually her brother. He was given nine months in Tennessee, then sent to South Carolina where he was promptly thrown into solitary. Just when it seemed things couldn't get worse, the FBI charged Gaskins with driving a stolen car over state lines, earning him another three years in federal prison in Atlanta, Georgia.

Life on the inside of the federal prison was slow and monotonous. There was very little freedom for the inmates who spent most of the day in their cells, lying in their bunks or wandering outside in the prison yard. And worst of all, there was no chance of escape. But Pee Wee made the most the most of his time there, cavorting with mafia goons and honing his skills as a criminal. He fondly called the three-year stretch his "college education."

By the time he was released from the federal penitentiary in August 1961, Gaskins had already spent a substantial portion of his young life in reform schools and prison. He had probably never worked an honest day in his life, and he wasn't about to start. For the next two years, Gaskins went to work for circuit-riding preacher George Todd, driving the minister's van and serving as his general assistant. Along the way, he broke into dozens of homes, stealing money, televisions, jewelry and anything else he could get his hands on. It was during this time that Pee Wee met his third wife, a seventeen-year-old that he considered over the hill.

Despite the surface placidity of his new life, Pee Wee's sexual depravity continued and within a month of his marriage, he was jailed for the statutory rape of a twelve-year-old girl in Florence County. While waiting for his arraignment, Gaskins jumped from a second-floor window at the Florence County Courthouse and disappeared into the swamps, evading capture for

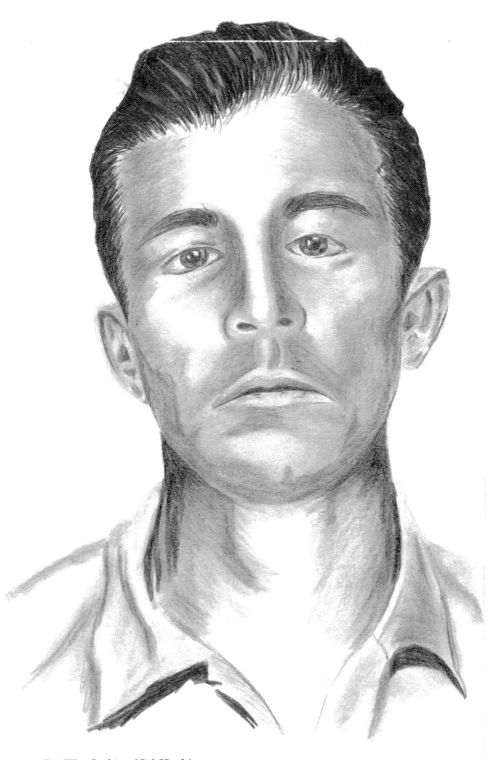

Pee Wee Gaskins. *Nick Hendrix*.

weeks. When bloodhounds finally had him cornered, Pee Wee caught the dogs and tied them to a tree. In his most audacious act, he snuck out of the swamps to write his name in the dust on an occupied police cruiser before fleeing north to Greensboro, North Carolina. Though still married to two of his other wives, in Greensboro he married his fourth, another seventeen-year-old girl. Within three months, he abandoned her, claiming that "I got so edgy and mad at the world, I just had to get away."

Heading to Georgia in a stolen car, Gaskins reunited with his third wife. They were traveling south toward Florida when a highway patrolman stopped them for speeding. Pee Wee had no intention of going back to jail. He left his wife to the police and fled to a nearby swamp, disappearing into the woods before the frantic officer could catch him. He reemerged to steal another car and again headed to North Carolina and wife number four. The police were waiting on him there, and he was taken into custody and returned to Florence where he received a six-year sentence for the rape charge and two more for the escape.

It was 1964 when Pee Wee was returned to the state pen, now renamed the Central Correctional Institute. Because of his reputation, Gaskins was able to run a pawnshop of sorts from his cell, pushing drugs, trafficking in contraband and arranging sexual favors. Incredibly, Pee Wee escaped from prison again in 1966 when he was on an outside work detail. He snatched the first motorist who came along Main Street from his car and fled. He was caught shortly thereafter and was never allowed on the outside again during the rest of his stay at CCI. In November 1968, Pee Wee was released from prison on the condition that he stay out of Florence for two years. "I was damned determined I never was going back to prison—which didn't meant that I wasn't ever going to do anything illegal again. I just wasn't never planning on getting caught," he later said. But he was wrong.

After his release, Gaskins went to work as a thief, stealing and stripping cars at a garage in Sumter, South Carolina. But he found that it was almost impossible to concentrate; he was consumed by those "bothersome feelings" that had plagued him his whole life. Soon thereafter, he started cruising the highway between Myrtle Beach and Charleston, looking for something he couldn't quite put his finger on. It would not take him long to find it.

In the late 1960s, hitchhikers were still a common sight on the highways, thumbing rides to Charleston or Florida. In September 1969, Gaskins stopped to pick up a young blonde girl hitchhiking from Myrtle Beach to

Charleston. When she rebuffed his sexual advances with a laugh, he drove her to an old logging road between Georgetown and Charleston where he beat her into submission. At that moment, everything seemed so simple—"a beam of light, like a vision" he later recalled. He brutally raped and sodomized the girl over the course of several hours then mutilated her as she begged for her life. When he had enough, he tied a chain onto her body and carried her to a nearby swamp. There, not a hundred yards from the logging road, Gaskins dumped his victim into the water and waited to see how long she could hold her breath. That moment proved to be life changing. "I felt truly the best I ever remembered feeling in my whole life," he would later say.

Slowly, methodically, still burglarizing and stealing cars along the way, Gaskins roamed the coastal highways in search of his next victim, and the perfect, isolated spot to take his victims. Sometime in late 1969 Gaskins found an old shack in the Lowcountry swamps. That's when the killing began in earnest.

Between 1969 and 1975, Gaskins went on a killing binge that cost dozens of men, women and children their lives. Most were female hitchhikers and runaways. Pee Wee's ritual for luring, murdering and disposing of his victims was generally the same. He offered a ride and then handcuffed his victims at knifepoint. Once bound, they were then tortured, raped and sodomized. Gaskins experimented with various cruelties that kept his victims screaming for days. How he actually ended their lives depended on his mood. Bludgeoning, stabbing, strangling, beating, drowning and dismemberment were all in his repertoire.

Gaskins cannibalized some of his victims, a ritual that is not unusual among serial killers. The first time he claimed to have done so was with a pair of teenagers he found hitchhiking along Highway 17. The two boys were weary from a day of walking and seemed happy to accept a ride with no special destination in mind. No sooner had they entered the car than Gaskins showed them his pistol. Once he got them to his hideout near Charleston, Gaskins kept them alive for nearly two days, sodomizing them and cannibalizing their genitals as they screamed in agony.

Sixteen-year-old Ann Colberson held a special place in Pee Wee's memory, perhaps because he kept her alive for so long before finally killing her. Pee Wee picked Ann up outside of Myrtle Beach in 1971 and took her to his hideaway. For four days he subjected her to the most ghoulish tortures that his mind could imagine, all the while promising that he would eventually let her go. That, of course, was never going to happen. He bludgeoned her with a hammer, slashed her throat and dumped her corpse in quicksand.

Though Gaskins was similar to more well-known murderers such as Ted Bundy and Jeffrey Dahmer, he was not a textbook serial killer. Serial killers usually target a specific type of victim—Bundy preferred young brunettes; Dahmer hunted young gay men. Gaskins was more complex than that. His victims fell under several categories: men, women and children that he killed for psycho-sexual pleasure; criminal associates who threatened his freedom; contract hits; and people who just pissed him off. The coastal killings were amusing to Gaskins, but he referred to the crimes that involved people he knew as his "serious murders."

One night in November 1970, Gaskins was out bumming around when he ran into his fifteen-year-old niece, Janice Kirby, and her seventeen-year-old friend, Patricia Allsbrook. The girls had been drinking and accepted a ride from Pee Wee. Gaskins had often entertained fantasies of sex with Janice but the opportunity had never really presented itself like this. He took both girls to an abandoned tenant house and ordered both to strip. The girls fought for their lives, but Gaskins was too strong and too vicious. He beat them unconscious with the butt of his pistol then murdered both girls. He stuffed Patricia in what he called "a cement pit," but thought it unseemly to leave his dead niece in a septic tank. He carried Janice's body out of the house and buried her behind an abandoned barn, then covered the ground with pine straw.

A few months later, Gaskins committed another "serious murder." The victim was Martha Dicks, a harmless braggart that he affectionately called "Clyde." Though Pee Wee was occasionally annoyed by Dicks, he let her hang around his garage, telling jokes and flirting with him. Dicks started telling people that she and Pee Wee were intimate and that she was pregnant with his child. That joke was enough for a death sentence. Gaskins killed her with chemicals he'd pilfered from a photographer after hearing him caution folks, "Don't never handle this stuff up here. It would kill you if you did." Gaskins poured a strong dose of the liquid into a drink of Coca-Cola. "She turned it up to her head and the next thing I knowed, the bottle hit the floor." He shoved the body in the backseat of his car, then discarded it in a ditch.

In the fall of 1971, Gaskins moved his family to Charleston to pursue a career in stolen military weaponry sales. He chose to live in a part of Charleston that boasted some of the city's most notorious scoundrels. Surrounded by other criminals, Gaskins felt right at home. He soon infiltrated the inner circle of criminality, becoming a man to be feared in the world of graft and larceny. He also returned to his coastal killings. Within three months of moving, he had raped, tortured and killed three more victims. Among those murdered was fourteen-year-old runaway Jackie Freeman. Gaskins subjected the girl to two days of rape, sodomy and cannibalism before mercifully ending her life.

After the murder of Freeman, Gaskins bought a purple hearse to ride around in. He ornamented it with a plastic skeleton hanging from the rearview mirror and a sign that read: WE HAUL ANYTHING, LIVING OR DEAD. When neighbors questioned why he would drive something so morose, Gaskins explained that he needed the hearse to haul bodies to his private cemetery. Nobody really took him seriously. But if the police had ever bothered to search the car, they would have discovered a shovel, handcuffs and enough forensic evidence to put Pee Wee on death row.

By Gaskins's account, the next to die were Johnny Sellers, thirty-six, and Jessie Ruth Judy, twenty-two, who owed Pee Wee money for getting Sellers out of jail. When Sellers was unable to pay off his debts, Pee Wee decided to kill him. He lured Johnny to a remote wooded area under the pretense that he had stashed stolen goods there. "Me and Johnny walked around there in the woods and I pretended I seen a snake, and I asked Johnny did he have his gun with him...So Johnny says, 'I ain't got no bullets for my gun.' I went back to my car and got my gun and I shot Johnny." Then he had to kill Jessie Judy, one of the few murders he ever regretted: "I took the knife out and I...said, 'Jessie, I'm gonna kill you.' Just like that, and she looked at me like she didn't believe it and...I said, 'I'm not kidding, Jessie. I really am.' And she still looked at me like she didn't believe it, and I just took it, stuck it right through...and she just wilted down to the ground, and I pulled the knife out." Gaskins hauled them both from Charleston to Prospect in the trunk of his car.

Gaskins said he next killed in 1973, when Doreen Dempsey, twenty-three, divorced and seven months' pregnant, arrived at his home in Prospect with her two-year-old daughter, Robin Michelle. Dempsey had stayed with Gaskins before and assumed she'd be welcome again. But this time, Gaskins decided he wanted sex for his generosity. Dempsey consented and began to undress, but when Pee Wee started undressing her daughter, Dempsey realized that he had other ideas. Before she could react, Gaskins bashed her head in with a hammer then raped, sodomized and strangled Robin Michelle. He initially claimed to authorities that he had murdered the child because she was the product of an interracial relationship. But that was a ruse. Years later, he would recall his brutal assault on Robin Michelle as the best sex of his life.

In the fall of 1975, Gaskins said, he decided to kill three "hippie types" whose van had broken down outside Georgetown. He offered the group a ride to town, taking the familiar detour to his shack in the Charleston swamps. With gun in hand, Gaskins sealed their lips with duct tape. After he handcuffed them, Gaskins said he raped and tortured the trio. "It was hard to say which one suffered most," he later recalled in his memoirs. Tired of the torture and mutilation, Pee Wee resorted to his old method of killing by sinking them in a Lowcountry swamp.

Gaskins knew he couldn't just leave the van sitting on the side of the road, so he recruited dimwitted ex-con Walter Neely to help take the van back to his shop in Prospect. Gaskins had always worked alone, and his decision to make an exception with Neely would eventually prove to be his undoing.

On February 12, 1975, Gaskins was hired by twenty-seven-year-old Suzanne "Long Legs" Kipper to kidnap and murder wealthy Florence farmer Silas Barnwell Yates. Kipper was angry with Yates after he broke off their affair, and with it her lavish lifestyle. Gaskins recruited Diane Neely, Walter's ex-wife, to lure Yates from his home claiming her car had broken down. When Yates walked out of the house, Pee Wee was waiting in the darkness with a gun. Gaskins claims to have stolen $2,100 from Yates's house before driving to Williamsburg County where Yates was killed and buried. Although Yates was believed to have been knifed to death, Gaskins claimed for years that he had crushed Yates's windpipe with a karate chop. After an autopsy in 1978, Pee Wee was furious when forensic evidence refuted that claim. "If you'll get somebody to bring the stuff, I'd show you that I can bust one-inch boards with my hand," he said. "His windpipe and all was busted. I think I could take that tape player right there and nearly about pop it in two with my hands."

A few months after the murder of Yates, Diane Neely and ex-convict Avery Howard decided to extort $5,000 out of Pee Wee in exchange for their silence about the murder. They had no idea who they were dealing with. When they arrived at the arranged meeting place, Gaskins was waiting with a .45 Beretta and a shovel. He reckoned that nobody would care if a couple of low-lifes like Neely and Howard turned up missing. He was right.

But people did care about the disappearance of thirteen-year-old Kim Ghelkins. The girl had been a frequent visitor to Gaskins's home, and

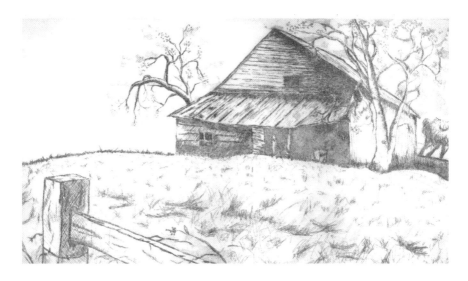

Pee Wee's graveyard. *Nick Hendrix.*

before her disappearance she told several people that Pee Wee and one of his friends had raped her. Pee Wee couldn't afford another rape charge, so he decided to get rid of the girl. He lured Ghelkins to a dirt road in rural Florence County, where he shot her in the back of the head, then stabbed her in the stomach. Asked why it was necessary to do both, Pee Wee flatly stated, "Well, I had my knife with me at the time."

Shortly thereafter, half-brothers Dennis Bellamy and Johnny Knight paid Gaskins a visit. They'd been looking for their missing sister Diane since April. With their questions threatening to draw attention to Diane Neely's disappearance, Gaskins took it upon himself to rectify the situation. One night while driving Dennis Bellamy around, Pee Wee pulled his car over in a wooded area to relieve himself. When Bellamy stepped out of the car, Gaskins shot him three times. With Bellamy dead, Pee Wee went back for Knight. "We was just walking on down there in the woods, and like I say, when I figured it was getting pretty close to where Dennis was at, I pulled my gun out and shot him, and that was all there was to it," he later recalled.

As Gaskins was tying up the loose ends in the Neely murder, police officers in North Charleston began investigating the disappearance of Kim Ghelkins. When they discovered that she had last been seen at Gaskins's home, it soon became obvious to the investigators that everywhere Gaskins lived—in Charleston, Florence, Sumter and

Williamsburg Counties—people disappeared. And Pee Wee was the "common thread that ran between them all." The authorities knew that an old crook like Gaskins couldn't be tricked into a confession, so they turned their attention to Walter Neely, Gaskins's dim-witted accomplice in the hippie murders. When detectives told him that his part in Ghelkins's murder might mean a date with the electric chair, Neely broke down and told them everything he knew, including the location of Pee Wee's graveyard.

Digging began Thursday, December 4, 1975, and by dusk, three bodies, including Bellamy's and Knight's, had been found. By Saturday the authorities had uncovered the remains of Doreen Dempsey and her two-year-old daughter, Johnny Sellers, Diane Neely, Kim Ghelkins and Barnwell Yates. Nine bodies were eventually unearthed, most buried two to a grave.

Gaskins was arrested while trying to flee and charged with eight counts of murder, though he repeatedly hinted that he had killed more, holding the location of the bodies until the day he would need to bargain for a stay of execution. Both Neely and Gaskins were sentenced to die for their crimes in May of 1976, but their sentences were commuted to life in prison when South Carolina's death penalty was overturned by the U.S. Supreme Court later that year.

But Gaskins wasn't going to let prison get in the way of his killing. Under contract from a relative of two of the murder victims of fellow inmate Rudolph Tyner, Gaskins rigged a phony intercom system with C-4 explosive into Tyner's cell. When the gullible Tyner plugged the system into the wall socket, the detonation caused his head to explode, scattering brain matter around the room. Pee Wee thought murdering Tyner was great fun, but it proved to be a fatal mistake. By then, the death penalty had been reinstated in South Carolina, and the authorities were not about to let this chance pass them by. Gaskins drew the death penalty again when he was convicted for Tyner's murder in 1982.

Pee Wee was tossed into solitary confinement for three years. When he emerged from his stretch in the hole, Gaskins became a celebrity with the local media. He even proposed to a news reporter he fancied. "I couldn't possibly marry you, Pee Wee," she said. "You've been married six times, and I'm Catholic." He also offered his solution to overcrowding in South Carolina's correctional system to a Charleston newspaper editor: "There are plenty of islands, such as a desert island 650 miles from Tahiti. Just send life-term and death inmates there, myself included.

I've got 23 people ready to leave tomorrow...We could farm, grow the food we eat, and it would save the state millions of dollars."

Gaskins filled his last months reading his memoirs to author Wilton Earl, eventually published as the book *Final Truth* in 1993. Beginning in rural Florence County where he was born, Gaskins gave the details of his life of murder and depravity. From the time he was sent to the South Carolina Industrial School for Boys until the time he arrived on death row, there were thousands of crimes and dozens of murders. Nobody will ever know how much of what was relayed to Earl's tape recorder was true. Many believe that Gaskins's death-row confessions were another lie, a grotesque elaboration of his growing reputation as South Carolina's most prolific killer. Pee Wee certainly had the capacity to kill, that much is certain. But only he knew how many really died.

Though he repeatedly tried to escape his date with "Old Sparky," South Carolina's pet name for the electric chair, he knew time was running out and he grew thoughtful as he told his story to Earl:

> *I am one of the few that truly understands what death and pain are all about...I have walked the same path as God. By taking lives and making others afraid of me, I become God's equal. Through killing others, I become my own Master. Through my own power I come to my own redemption. Once I seen the miracle light, I didn't never again have to fear or obey the Rules of no Man or no God...I'm not asking nobody's forgiveness. I got no apologies to make for my life. I always had my reasons for everything I've ever done...When they put me to death, I'll die remembering the freedom and pleasure of my life. I'll die knowing that there are others coming along to take my place, and that most of them won't never get caught.*

As crowds gathered outside the prison walls chanting, "Burn, Pee Wee, Burn!" Donald Henry Gaskins was executed at 1:05 a.m. on September 6, 1991.

MASSACRE IN
MOUNT PLEASANT

On the evening of December 20, 1978, copy editor for the *News and Courier* Grace Kutkus was working on the first edition of the paper when the phone rang. She figured it was someone asking about a sports score or looking for the circulation department. But the next fifteen minutes would be like something out of the most outlandish fiction.

"I'm Pete Davis, and I've just murdered three people in Mount Pleasant," the man said in a calm and emotionless voice.

Wondering if she had a crank caller on the phone, Kutkus said nothing. Instinctively recognizing her doubt, the caller said she should call the police to confirm his story. He even had the number handy. He also wanted to get the call underway because he claimed to have ingested a lethal dose of poison and had only a few minutes to live. As the caller chatted away, Kutkus motioned editor Bill Bryan to her desk and pointed to a note detailing the conversation. The police were called and every effort was made to keep Davis talking as the phone number was traced.

Over the next several minutes, the caller revealed that he was a local attorney and that he had killed his ex-girlfriend, Elaine Robinson, less than an hour earlier at her home in Mount Pleasant. "Then I killed her mother and her stepfather," he said. He claimed that they were Helen and Joe Sharpton and that the police could find their bodies at 1060

North Shem Drive. "They're all dead. At least I did all I could to kill them," he told Kutkus.

Standing at a payphone, Davis explained that Robinson had him arrested a few days earlier for burglary and domestic abuse. "They probably wouldn't have released me if they knew I was insane," he added with a laugh. Fearing that his career was now destroyed, he purchased a shotgun three days later. "I'd never used one, and they tried to show me how to use it at the store," he told Kutkus. Though she was shaken by what he said, Kutkus frantically took down every word while the reporters worked to confirm the story.

The last three minutes of the conversation were recorded and printed in the *News and Courier*:

> *DAVIS: I'm really getting too sick to talk.*
> *KUTKUS: Well, is there anything else you want to tell us?*
> *DAVIS: Let me think. I disagree with the policy in Far East Asia!*
> *[laughs] No, no, nothing like that.*
> *KUTKUS: Who was the 10-year-old boy you think you might have shot?*
> *DAVIS: Well, it was, see, Elaine my chick, she, ah, has this boy that won't live with her and, ah, I didn't know it and I came through the glass door with the shotgun.*
> *KUTKUS: You came through the glass door at her house?*
> *DAVIS: Yeah. Her mother's house...he won't live with her. I came through the door with the ah, with the, ah, with the shotgun and the door didn't just break out, it shattered. And I couldn't see. And, ah, I shot Joe because he's, he's, he's nothing. He's nothing at all. "RAAAAAA!" he hollered, you know. I'm not trying to be morbid or nothing like that. She started running toward me and said, "You son-of-a-bitch." I shot her one time and I thought I shot...*
> *KUTKUS: Was that Elaine, that you shot?*
> *DAVIS: No, no, Elaine was at her house.*
> *KUTKUS: Oh. You shot her first?*
> *DAVIS: Her mother and her stepfather, Joe Sharpton were at the other house. With the little boy. And I certainly hope I didn't hurt the little boy. He's got a lot of emotional problems. That doesn't make any difference, I just didn't want to shoot him. But Elaine... Elaine...I was charged with burglary for breaking into her house and fighting with her. Lt. Walker gets carried away with himself as do the Mount Pleasant police and Judge Stith over on Sullivan's*

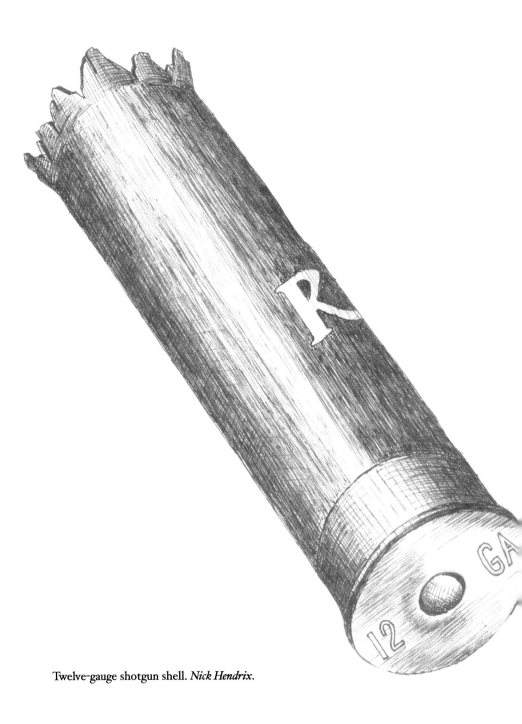

Twelve-gauge shotgun shell. *Nick Hendrix*.

Island. [laughter] *They accepted the case and he let me out on bond. I guess he was wrong because he didn't know I was insane.*

KUTKUS: *When was it that you were arrested and charged with burglary?*

DAVIS: *Last Sunday I think.*

KUTKUS: *Sunday?*

DAVIS: *Yeah.*

KUTKUS: *Well, why did you go to the Sharptons'?*

DAVIS: *Right after I shot Elaine.*

KUTKUS: *No, why though?*

DAVIS: *To kill them!*

KUTKUS: *To kill her mother?*

DAVIS: *Yeah, and her stepfather.*

KUTKUS: *Had they been involved in the trouble you all were having?*

DAVIS: *Oh God yeah. Busybodies. I got to go. I'm getting real sick and I need to take some more medicine to die. And I appreciate you listening to me.*

KUTKUS: *Well, Mr. Davis, you don't have to die...*

DAVIS: *Listen, don't give me all that stuff, man...I'd be in prison...*

KUTKUS: *Well, it's true...no...there are people...*

DAVIS: *I've got to go, I'm getting sick. Thank you very much for listening.*

KUTKUS: *OK.*

DAVIS: *Bye.*

REPORTER EDWARD FENNELL: *Hello?*

DAIVS: *Hello.*

FENNELL: *Hello?*

DAVIS: *I've already talked all I want to, man. You'll have to listen to your chick...ok, bye.*

FENNELL: *Well, ah...*

[Click—Brrrrrrrrrrrrrrr...]

FENNELL: *Oh my God!*

The Mount Pleasant police department had received a call earlier that evening from a concerned neighbor about a possible shooting at 3 Ellen Drive. Neighbor John Rosell was riding his bike when he saw Davis pull into the driveway. He said that Davis walked to the front door with a shotgun, the sales tag still hanging from the barrel. "He tried the door

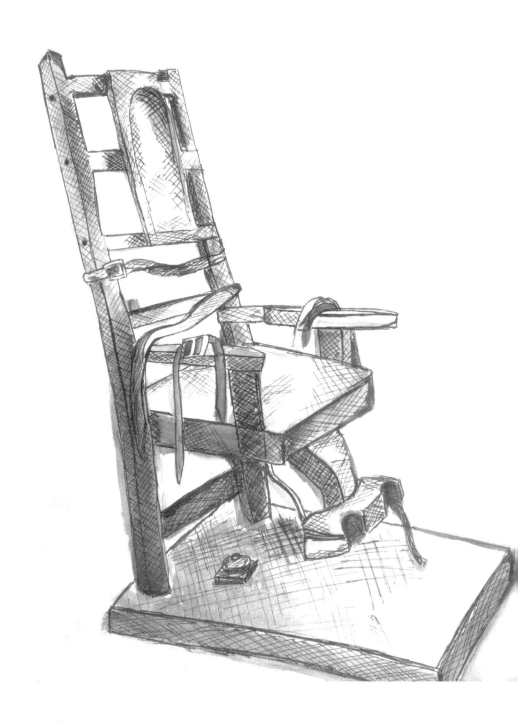

Old Sparky. *Sandra Hayden*.

and it was locked...he went to the front window and said 'open the door.' Then he smashed the window," Rosell said. Rosell tried to call the police, but it was too late. He heard a shot, then a minute later, two more. According to witnesses, Davis stayed in the house several minutes then fled in his 1972 Ford pickup.

As the officers turned into the driveway at 3 Ellen Drive, they had no way of knowing the horror they were about to witness, an image of carnage that would stay with them for the rest of their lives. Upon entering the house, they found Elaine Robertson lying dead in her living room. She had no vital signs and it was apparent that she had died as a result of a shotgun blast. The officers also discovered Robertson's roommate, who had been home when Davis broke in. She fell to the floor during the attack, and fortunately for her, Davis believed she was dead.

At about the same time, another police cruiser was sent to the Sharptons' home as a precautionary measure. The officers were greeted by a nightmarish scene: the rooms were blood-spattered and riddled with buckshot, and the smell of fresh gunpowder still saturated the air. They soon discovered two corpses, one in the kitchen and one in the living room. Davis had been telling the truth on the phone. Elaine Robertson's mother and stepfather were also dead.

Unsure whether the perpetrator was still in the general vicinity, the officers immediately called for backup before moving past the bodies to search the rest of the house. Hoping to spot the gunman in the home, they shined their lights around the interior. They didn't find the gunman, but they did find Mrs. Robinson's nine-year-old son lying on the couch. He was uninjured.

Police cordoned off all routes out of the city, determined to find their murder suspect. They also began to look into the circumstances of the killing. From the start, it was obvious that the accused killer had been falling apart for months before the murders. According to Davis's secretary, Margaret Lancaster, during the year leading up to the tragedy, Pete Davis's mental state had greatly declined. When he was arrested five days before the murders, he became withdrawn and worried that his legal practice was in jeopardy. "He pointed to those certificates on the wall and said, 'Margaret, I worked hard for those...to get where I am. Now it looks like I'm going to lose it all,'" she said.

He seemed to snap out of his funk the afternoon before the killings. He even seemed happy as he talked to clients and visited colleagues in a nearby office. But everything seemed to fall apart when he received a call late that afternoon. He left the office and never returned.

Seven days after the triple murder, Alvin Simmons, his brother Robert Simmons Jr., Raymond Dilligard and James Sneed were out hunting with deer dogs when they ran across a pickup truck parked along an old logging road outside Awendaw. As they approached the truck, they saw a man lying face down beside the back wheel. It was obvious that he had been dead for days. With news reports broadcasting the details of the murders for nearly eight days, there was no doubt who the dead man was. When law enforcement officials from Mount Pleasant, Charleston and the FBI arrived, they found a fully loaded shotgun in the front seat of the truck. An unloaded .22-caliber was also found in the cab along with two bottles of wine, a few cans of beer and four unspent shotgun shells. Detectives discovered a bottle of lithium carbonate in Davis's front pocket.

BIBLIOGRAPHY

Butterfield, Fox. *All God's Children: The Boskett Family and the American Tradition of Violence*. New York: Harper Collins, 1996.

Clark, Culpepper. *Francis W. Dawson and the Politics of Restoration*. Tuscaloosa: University of Alabama Press, 1980.

Coclanis, Peter. *Shadow of a Dream: Economic Life and Death in the South Carolina Low Country 1670–1920*. New York: Oxford University, 1989.

Covington, James W. "Stuart's Town. The Yemassee Indians and Spanish Florida." *The Florida Anthropologist* 21 (1978): 8–13.

DePratter, Chester B. "The Chiefdom of Cofitachequi." In *The Forgotten Centuries: Indians and Europeans in the American South, 1521–1704*, edited by Charles Hudson and Carmen Tesser, 197–226. Athens: University of Georgia Press, 1994.

———."The Juan Pardo Expeditions: North from Santa Elena." *Southeastern Archaeology* 9, no. 2:140–46.

DePratter, Chester B., Charles Hudson, and Marvin T. Smith. "The Route of Juan Pardo's Explorations in the Interior Southeast, 1566–1568." *Florida Historical Quarterly* 62, no. 2 (1983): 125–58.

Dobyns, Henry F. *Their Number Become Thinned: Native American Population Dynamics in Eastern North America*. Knoxville: University of Tennessee Press, 1983.

Edgar, Walter B. *Partisans and Redcoats: the Southern Conflict that Turned the Tide of the American Revolution*. New York: Harper Collins, 2001.

———. *South Carolina: A History*. Columbia: University of South Carolina Press, 1998.

Edgar, Walter B., and N. Louise Bailey. *Biographical Directory of the South Carolina House of Representatives: Volume II, The Commons House of Assembly, 1692–1775*. Columbia: University of South Carolina Press, 1977.

Ferguson, Leland. *Uncommon Ground: Archaeology and Early African America 1650-1800*. Washington, DC: Smithsonian Institution Press, 1992.

Fraser, George MacDonald. *The Steel Bonnets: The Story of the Anglo-Scottish Border Reivers*. Oxford, England: Akadine Press, 2001.

Fraser, Walter. *Charleston! Charleston! The History of a Southern City*. Columbia: University of South Carolina Press, 1989.

Frost, John. *An Illustrated History of North America, From the Earliest Period to the Present Time*. New York: Published by Henry Bill, 1860.

Garden, Alexander. *A Brief Account of the Deluded Dutartres*. New Haven, 1762.

Gaskins, Donald H. with Wilton Earle. *Final Truth: The Autobiography of a Serial Killer*. Star, SC: Adept Books, 1992.

Gregorie, Anne K. *Christ Church 1706–1959: A Plantation Parish of the South Carolina Establishment*. Charleston: The Dalcho Historical Society, 1961.

Harvin, Stephanie. "Hunters Discovered Corpse." *The News and Courier*, December 28, 1978.

Hewat, Alexander. *An Historical Account of the Rise and Progress of the Colonies of South Carolina and Georgia*. 2 vols. London, 1779; reprint: Spartanburg, SC: The Reprint Co., 1962.

"Horrid Massacre in Virginia." Woodcut illustration in *Authentic and Impartial Narrative of the Tragical Scene Which Was Witnessed in Southampton County*. 1831. Prints and Photographs Division, Library of Congress.

Joyner, Charles. *Down by the Riverside: A South Carolina Slave Community*. Urbana and Chicago: University of Illinois Press, 1985.

Klein, Rachel N. *Unification of a Slave State: The Rise of the Planter Class in the South Carolina Backcountry, 1760–1808*. Chapel Hill: University of North Carolina Press, 1990.

Klingberg, Frank J. *The Carolina Chronicle of Dr. Francis Le Jau, 1706–1717*. Berkeley: University of California Press, 1956.

Kutkus, Grace. "Caller Says He Killed 3." *The News and Courier*, December 21, 1973.

Lambert, Robert S. *South Carolina Loyalists in the American Revolution*. Columbia: University of South Carolina Press, 1987.

Lawrence S. Rowland, Alexander Moore, and George C. Rogers. *The History of Beaufort County, South Carolina: 1514–1861*. Columbia: University of South Carolina Press, 1996.

Laylon Wayne Jordan, and Elizabeth H. Stringfellow. *A Place Called St. John's: The Story of John's, Edisto, Wadmalaw, Kiawah, and Seabrook Islands of South Carolina*. Spartanburg, SC: The Reprint Company, 1998.

Lumpkin, Henry. *From Savannah to Yorktown: The American Revolution in the South*. Columbia: University of South Carolina Press, 1981.

McCrady, Edward. *The History of South Carolina in the Revolution, 1775–1780*. New York: Macmillan Company, 1901.

———. *The History of South Carolina Under the Proprietary Government, 1670–1719*. New York: Macmillan Company, 1897.

McCurry, Stephanie. *Masters of Small Worlds: Yeoman Households, Gender Relations, and the Political Culture of the Antebellum South Carolina Low Country*. New York: Oxford University Press, 1995.

The News and Courier, "Tape Reveals Final Minutes of Call," December 28, 1978.

Pancake, John S. *This Destructive War: The British Campaign in the Carolinas, 1780–1782*. Tuscaloosa: University of Alabama Press, 1985.

Public Broadcasting Service. "The American Experience: The History of Dueling in America." Available at http://www.pbs.org/wgbh/amex/duel/sfeature/dueling.html.

Ravenel, Beatrice St. Julien, ed. *Charleston Murders*. New York: Duel, Sloan and Pierce, 1947.

———. *Charleston: The Place and the People*. New York: Macmillan, 1906.

Sabine, Lorenzo. *Notes on Duels and Dueling*. Boston: Crosby, Nichols and Company, 1992.

Salley, A.S. Jr., ed. *Warrants for Lands in South Carolina 1672–1711*. Columbia: University of South Carolina Press, 1973.

Sirmans, M. Eugene. *Colonial South Carolina: A Political History, 1663–1763*. Chapel Hill: University of North Carolina Press, 1966.

Smith, Henry A.M. *The Historical Writings of Henry A.M. Smith*. Spartanburg: The Reprint Company, 1988.

The State, "In Cold Blood," September 1, 1991.

———. "A Life of Death," September 5, 1991.

Thomas, W.H.J. "Dueling Once Popular in Lowcountry." *The News and Courier*, January 6, 1968.

Waddell, Eugene. *Indians of the South Carolina Low Country, 1562–1751*. Spartanburg: The Reprint Company, 1980.

Weir, Robert M. *Colonial South Carolina, A History*. New York: KTO Press, 1983.

Williams, Jack Kenny. *Vogues in Villany*. Columbia: University of South Carolina Press, 1959.

Wood, Peter H. *Black Majority: Negroes in Colonial South Carolina from 1670 through the Stono Rebellion*. New York: Alfred A. Knopf, 1974.

Woodmason, Charles. *The Carolina Backcountry*. Chapel Hill: University of North Carolina Press, 1953.

W.P.A. *Archaeological Excavations in Chatham County, Georgia: 1937–1942*. Laboratory of Archaeology Series, No. 29. Athens: University of Georgia, 1991.